The Enneagram Unveiled

A Christian & Metaphysical Perspective

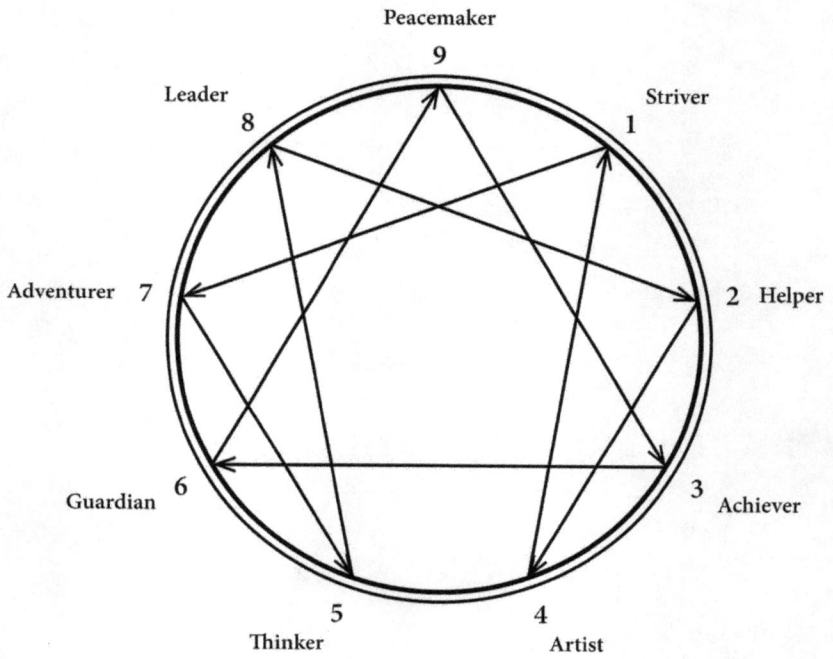

Peacemaker

9

Leader

8

Striver

1

Adventurer 7

2 Helper

Guardian 6

3 Achiever

5

4

Thinker

Artist

Thomas Garrett Isham

THE
ENNEAGRAM
UNVEILED

A Christian &
Metaphysical Perspective

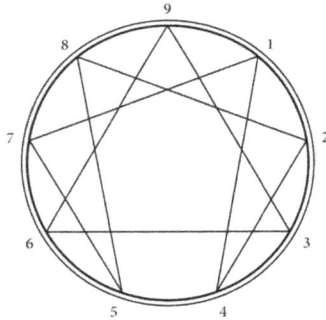

PHILOSOPHIA
PERENNIS

First published in
the USA by Sophia Perennis 2013
as *The Orthodox Enneagram*
Second, retitled edition
Philosophia Perennis 2017
© Thomas Garrett Isham 2013

Series editor: James R. Wetmore

For information, address:
Philosophia Perennis
84 Main St, Peterborough, NH 03458
jameswetmore@mac.com

978-1-62138-256-0 pb
978-1-62138-257-7 cloth
978-1-62138-258-4 ebook

Cover Design: Michael Schrauzer

CONTENTS

To Garrett and Adam,
with love and pride

Foreword

To be delivered by God, we must first be undeceived about ourselves.
~ St. Augustine of Hippo

TWO BASIC ENTITIES, the enneagram of personality types and metaphysical orthodoxy, are at the heart of the following pages. Throughout, these two entities complement one another. Remove one of them, and there is no book. A number of authors and teachers have expounded the enneagram after their own fashion, and not a few pioneering souls have recovered and elucidated the principles of traditional metaphysics. We are beholden to both groups. Neither group, however, has combined the enneagram with traditional metaphysics. This book does so.

That is, it explains the system of psychological and spiritual teaching known as the enneagram in the context of what is variously called traditional metaphysics, primordial wisdom, *religio perennis, sophia perennis,* or, quite simply, Tradition, with a capital "T." The goal is to integrate the riches of these two disciplines; one to explore the motivations of personality according to type, the other to ground personality in its microcosmic, macrocosmic and metacosmic dimensions. To have one without the other is, we believe, to limit one's ability to understand the human condition in both its immanent and transcendent modes; in its links to both temporal and timeless concerns.

This is not to imply that traditional metaphysics were in some way inadequate until buttressed by the relatively recent arrival of the enneagram. The enneagram is not a religion or a metaphysics, but primarily a discipline of the soul; it does not attempt to replace the organic wholeness of a transcendent doctrine. Nonetheless, it plays a special role in the present age, for it speaks an idiom that is readily understandable, given a measure of self-reflection and a wish to

I

master its basic ideas. This is a valuable contribution. Even better, it is grounded in traditional principles, and able to convey those principles to present-day sensibilities.

The enneagram and traditional metaphysics alike, in complementary ways, aim to rescue lost, drifting, confused, frustrated, empty, unbalanced, or, simply, generically dissatisfied souls, by which we mean . . . most everyone. They aim to rescue us, as it were, from the "human condition," from maladies of the soul that afflict everyone more or less frequently, despite outward appearances. Though the enneagram directs its therapeutic resources towards the soul (or *psyche*, the words mean the same thing), it recognizes the relationship between soul and *spirit,* as well as the spirit's link to transcendent domains.

In addition to drawing data from enneagram theory and traditional metaphysics, we draw on various non-traditional thinkers of more recent vintage, among them Immanuel Kant, C.G. Jung and Karen Horney. We do this owing to their psychological acumen, and from the privilege to collect honey from many flowers. Less sweetly, St. Augustine would have called it "spoiling the Egyptians," that is, claiming the use of "heathen" wisdom.[1] In his view, God had scattered "gold and silver" throughout creation, whence it had been mined by diligent sages from the earliest days. In turn, Christians were within their rights to mine this precious ore as well. In our case, we partly draw from a modern deposit, wherein fruitful knowledge has been stored, despite deficient views underlying its content.

The metaphysical framework we use is not meant to constrain but to liberate, even as truth itself liberates. To be sure, the framework establishes limits, but within those limits there is ample freedom in which to navigate one's life. It is the absence of such a framework that proves, sooner or later, to be itself a limiting and inhibiting condition, for lack of boundaries sends the unwary into a ditch or off a cliff. A singular writer once spoke of orthodoxy in

---

1. Taken from Exodus 12:35–38, in which the Israelites, on leaving captivity, "plundered the Egyptians" of their silver and gold jewelry and of their clothes. Interestingly, Moses, raised as a prince of Egypt, was himself "learned in all the wisdom of the Egyptians" (Acts 7:22), thus a borrower himself of pagan spiritual lore.

comparable terms, imagining a group of children playing on the flat, grassy top of a tall island in the sea. So long as there was a wall around the cliff's edge, the children could fling themselves into every possible game, and make the place the happiest of playgrounds. But the walls were knocked down, leaving them in peril of the precipice. "They did not fall over; but when their friends returned to them they were all huddled in terror in the centre of the island; and their song had ceased."[2]

Walls, boundaries, frameworks: These can be liberating. The framework used here, we believe, is congruent with who we are as persons; not who we are on the surface, but who we are in our deepest, truest selves. By using it, we are able to understand and penetrate our essential nature, lest we be trapped in our false nature, thus facing imminent or ultimate frustration, or both. "You have made us for yourself, O Lord, and our heart is restless until it rests in you" (St. Augustine again).

We do not place ourselves in a "box" by seeking to understand our essential nature after the manner of traditional metaphysics, or by assigning ourselves a number on the enneagram. The fact is, by nature we are *in* a box, a box partly of our own making; trapped in our wounded natures and in need of liberation. Traditional metaphysics, by defining and describing the multi-layered reality in which we are encased, and the enneagram, by defining and describing the insufficient strategies we employ to survive and flourish in that reality, are means by which to escape from the box.

Says a metaphysician of note: "Detailed knowledge of the determining forces to which one is subject can open the way to a new freedom, since the most dangerous influences are the ones which operate unnoticed."[3] The enneagram answers to this idea, for it exposes the hidden agendas of persons of every type, in a manner that is indeed detailed. By doing so, it clarifies one's psychological

---

2. G. K. Chesterton, *Orthodoxy* (Image Books, a Division of Doubleday & Company, Inc., Garden City, New York, 1959), 145.

3. Robert Bolton, *Keys of Gnosis* (Sophia Perennis, Hillsdale, New York, 2004), 111–112. Although the author is not affiliated with the enneagram, his insight harmonizes with it.

nature in its many expressions, while demonstrating its potential for integration into one's spiritual or transcendent nature.

We write from a Christian perspective, but are mindful of the wisdom to be culled from the full spectrum of the primordial tradition. For doctrines both East and West carry within themselves the spiritual wisdom of the race; they carry the metaphysical intuitions that underlie every religion or spiritual philosophy, intuitions that prefigure and determine every exoteric presentation of transcendent verities. By employing perennial doctrine in conjunction with the subtle technique of the enneagram, we believe both an explanation and an antidote are provided to meet our deepest needs.

1

The Orthodox Enneagram

*If an idea is true it belongs equally to all those capable of understanding it;
if it is false there is no reason to be proud of having thought it A true idea
cannot be 'new,' since truth is not a product of the human mind; the truth
exists independently of ourselves, and it is for us simply to comprehend it;
outside of this knowledge there can be nothing but error.*

$\sim$ René Guénon

As INDICATED in the Foreword, we intend to present in a new key the spiritual and psychological dimensions of the enneagram of personality types, within an orthodox or traditional framework.

Why "orthodox?" Because orthodox or traditional doctrines are, in our view, quite simply true, and no greater recommendation can be made for them. But "what is truth?" one might ask, echoing the words of a certain imperial official of two millennia past. What is meant by these terms will, we hope, be made clear as we proceed, for otherwise, our claims will surely be found implausible by our contemporaries, and if not considered an affront to the intellect, perhaps an expression of arrogance and bad manners.

In brief, we adhere to what is called *metaphysical* orthodoxy, to principles that transcend the limitations of the ego, to principles that provide the order and structure that reveals to the ego the path that leads to psychological and spiritual liberation.

To be clear: "orthodoxy," in this context, refers not to Eastern Orthodox Christianity, nor to Roman Catholic or Protestant orthodoxies, nor to any other religious orthodoxies that might come to mind, but, again, to *metaphysical* orthodoxy, that is, to a philosophical doctrine that allows man to make non-empirical reality intelligible to himself. Although this approach does not in the least dismiss the various religious orthodoxies, it does in fact put metaphysical principles first, a tactic that adapts itself admirably, we believe, to the purposes of this discussion. This is because metaphysical principles underlie every authentic religious expression, whether acknowledged or not, even as they underlie the various sacred sciences and symbolisms that are universally valid. In our view, it is less a question of consulting first and foremost the various sacred writings of the world than of showing the universal principles that underlie them, principles that express the integral coherence of traditional teachings as a whole, and their relevance to the enneagram.

Although special revelation is expressed by way of religious scriptures, there is nonetheless—according to certain metaphysical and religious authorities—an unwritten primordial tradition that spread from Paradise with the scattering of peoples on the earth, in the aftermath of the Catastrophe or Fall recounted in the various mythologies of the world. It is that Catastrophe or Fall that placed mankind in the unnatural and unbalanced condition in which he finds himself to this day. On the heels of that Catastrophe, the primordial tradition—or rather, the divine power behind the primordial tradition—began its reparative work, revealing *exoterically* the pattern of the divine-human relationship and prescribing antidotes— rituals, laws, customs—to address mankind's chronically unsettled condition. Such revelations were enshrined in various scriptures, though interior or *esoteric* teachings were abroad as well. This second category of teachings pointed to the truth embedded *in* man, a structure without which sacred writings would find no template in which to reveal themselves. This interior structure was, and is, able to absorb and reflect the uncolored light of perennial gnosis, and is the substance of esoteric doctrines both past and present.

It is through this primordial light that one absorbs and reflects the various tints and hues of the sacred traditions. In the early narratives of the race, the light reflects itself in the spectrum of the rainbow, the sign that God gave Noah in the wake of the Deluge. The rainbow is the sign of God's covenant with all mankind, prior to the Abrahamic

covenant with the Hebrew people only.[4] The earlier covenant under-
lies and finds expression in various sacred traditions. Such varied
spiritual "languages," descended from primordial tradition itself,
provide a voice to the nations by which to express their link to the
Divine. In the words of Jean Borella,

> The rainbow appears when the sun, being behind the observer,
> casts its rays upon a rain cloud, the water droplets of which
> reflect these rays back to the observer, making them iridescent
> and splitting up the solar spectrum according to its various col-
> ors. To perceive the sign of the covenant is necessarily, then, to
> turn one's back to the white light of the sun, which no one can
> look at directly. We can only perceive this light refracted through
> the merciful veil of the rain and as a color gradient spread out
> from infrared to ultraviolet. The cloud, as we know, is a symbol
> of the divine presence; its dissolving into rain is a symbol of this
> presence becoming grace and descending on mankind.[5]

The sun's white light, then, split into various colors, signifies
God's revelation of himself by way of several sacred traditions, each
of which finds its root in a religious essence or archetype located in
the transcendent domain. It is not our intention to recommend a
universalist point of view, but to recognize the omnipresent hand
of God in the working out of mankind's spiritual destiny, by way
of a plurality of expressions. Even by using the measuring rod of
the Bible, one cannot summarily dismiss the claims of the revelations located outside that singular source.[6] Amidst the diversity of
expressions, we discern the Holy Spirit's "rain of grace," present in

---

4. Genesis 9:12–17.

5. Jean Borella, "The Problematic of the Unity of Religions," in *Sacred Web: A
Journal of Tradition and Modernity,* vol. 17, M. Ali Lakhani, publisher and editor
(North Vancouver, British Columbia, June 2006), 180. In his metaphor, Borella
refers to a passage from the first book of the Bible. Interestingly, in the last book of
the Bible, reference is made to a throne that "stood in heaven, with one seated on
the throne," and "around the throne was a rainbow" (Revelation 4:2–3).

6. The Bible makes clear the salvation of any number of Old Testament saints,
not to mention the salvation of righteous gentiles as well.

each to one degree or another. More to our purpose, we find a microcosmic reflection of this diversity in the spectrum of personality represented by the enneagram, where individuals of various types reflect in their essence the various colors of the "uncolored light" of the *imago Dei,* the wounded but intact image of God within their souls and spirits.[7]

There is in every sacred tradition a concept of *palingenesis* or rebirth, that is, a spiritual transmutation, by which men and women are given new life, new purpose, new power. They are—to use enneagram terminology—integrated into their spiritual core, having previously been imprisoned in the ego, in compulsive bondage to one besetting sin or another, estranged from their spiritual center and from the Divine element that resides within it. Yet even with the ego replaced on its pivot in the spiritual core, conscious life is not immediately affected; the faculties of thinking, feeling and willing remain largely as they were. Transmutation occurs only when the Spirit, having been "activated," begins bit by bit to reclaim the mind, by enlightenment; the heart, by inspiration, and the will, by strengthening. By the outworking of the Spirit, then, aided by

7. Some of the severest and most orthodox churchmen of earlier centuries have acknowledged the activity of divine wisdom and eternal salvation outside the Christian fold. The anti-revolutionary historian, Groen van Prinsterer, believed that "philosophy outside the pale of Christian revelation has historically given voice to truthful insights." Moreover, he accounted for this by saying that "all philosophies are derivations of religion and that all religions are derivations of the one true religion given to man—borrowings from the original, primordial revelation given in Paradise." (Harry van Dyke, *Groen van Prinsterer's Lectures on Unbelief and Revolution* [Wedge Publishing Foundation, Jordan Station, Ontario, 1989], 50). Another example, discovered at random, is the hymn writer Augustus Toplady, who claimed that "Undoubtedly, there are elect Jews, elect Mahometans, and elect Pagans. In a word, countless millions of persons whom Christ hath redeemed unto God, by his blood, out of every kindred, and tongue, and people, and nation (Rev. 5:9)." (*The Complete Works of Augustus Toplady* [Sprinkle Publications, Harrisonburg, Virginia, 1987], 811). This does not argue universal salvation, which, on the face of it, is opposed by the Bible, as well as other sacred texts. It does suggest that God is able, by ways unclear to our limited perspective, to pluck "like a brand from the fire" whomever he chooses. "How unsearchable are your judgments, how inscrutable your ways" (Romans 11:33).

means of disciplined reflection, these fragmented faculties achieve an inner rapport hitherto absent.

Let us return to the concept of metaphysical orthodoxy. Metaphysical orthodoxy (like religious orthodoxy, in its own sphere) means right doctrine, and right doctrine—that is, knowledge that is sound and correct—is vital to understanding human nature in both its psychological and spiritual domains, and, *inter clia,* in understanding the enneagram as it relates to both domains as well.

To speak of orthodoxy implies the existence of heterodoxy, the existence, that is, of conceptions at variance with the orthodox view. In the orthodox view, such conceptions are quite simply departures from correct and self-evident principles. To position oneself within a metaphysical system that is heretical, then, is to build with defective materials. To follow a religious ritual or a psychological practice that is equally defective is to risk perpetual enslavement to the ego. For the ego is, in the words of an eminent student of the inner life,

> a Hydra-headed monster sprouting two heads for each cut off, and it is [authentic] ritual alone that can cauterize the wound and prevent new growth, and at the same time nourish the soul with the legitimate food proper to its spiritual formation. Ritual is God's, as opposed to man's way. It is a medicine, an antidote to self-deception, a corrective, a restorative, a healing balm, a power outside of our own limitations, delegated by God. . . . Its usage differs following each revelation, each age and society, but its end is always the same, namely, a support capable of putting us in contact with the Divine Center, source of all Reality.[8]

Absent authentic spiritual form and method, we find ourselves in the position of the man in the Gospel who, having been freed of an unclean spirit, soon finds himself invaded by seven additional unclean spirits, each more evil than the first (Matthew 12:43–45). Such is the prospect for those who forgo authentic spiritual practice.

The goal of every authentic ritual is to put us into contact with

---

8. Whitall N. Perry, editor, *The Spiritual Ascent: A Compendium of the World's Wisdom* (Fons Vitae, Louisville, Kentucky, 2007), 272.

states of being that both surpass our individuality and bridge the gulf between lower and higher selves. Such states are realized at the personal and transpersonal *center* or *essence* of Being, wherein both horizontal and vertical lines intersect symbolically in the form of a cross. The horizontal line represents the psychological domain, spreading to left and right in increments of ever greater fragmentation and dispersal, while the vertical line represents the spiritual domain, on which rises and falls the human essence or center, moving towards greater or lesser spiritual realization.

It is the purpose of psychological and spiritual disciplines to reintegrate the horizontal and vertical displacements and disorders of psyche and essence. In traditional practice, it was the task of the Lesser Mysteries to achieve the first of these goals, the task of the Greater Mysteries to achieve the second. It is to the first of these that the enneagram initially applies, for it chiefly addresses the mind, heart and will of the psyche or soul, to help remedy the disorders of the ego. By doing so, however, it both unties the knots of the soul and makes supple the operation of the spiritual self, that is, the essential or core self.

By employing the enneagram, we address the maladies of our type and subtype; we swim against the currents of psychic energy; we seek the sources of spiritual illumination. To use another metaphor, we work "against the arrows"[9] to perform an *agere contra*, an "acting against." This leads to integration. It requires effort. By contrast, if we act "with the arrows," it is equivalent to swimming *with* the current, acquiescing in the tidal pull of disintegration.

The enneagram prescribes a method best identified as a form of *gnosis*, not to be confused with the heretical movements of the early Christian period. It is *gnosis* in its basic sense, that is, a form of mystical or spiritual knowledge, an "integrating knowledge" that grasps the relations between levels of reality, between, for example, God, humanity, and the universe.[10] It is a mode of knowing that is

9. Enneagram "arrows" will be discussed at various times in this volume.

10. *Gnosis* is a much misunderstood term, not least in Christian circles. According to Jean Borella (in *The Secret of the Christian Way: A Contemplative Ascent Through the Writings of Jean Borella,* edited and translated by G. John Champoux

different from "scientific" or "rational" knowing, though willing and able to use these in its procedures.[11]

For its part, the *gnosis* of the enneagram liberates the knower by uncovering patterns of interior motivation, by naming erstwhile unrecognized inner "demons." It frees a person from psychological ambushes that fragment and unsettle the soul. In doing so, it equilibrates the psyche and integrates it into Spirit. It does these things by means of grace, even as one exercises greater capacities for thinking, feeling and willing. In the end, it leads to a wisdom consisting essentially of two parts: knowledge of God and of ourselves.

[State University of New York Press, Albany, 2001]), major figures in church history have held a favorable view of it, rightly understood. He remarks, however, that his own studies "have unleashed an actual tempest. . . . Accustomed to seeing the term *gnosis* in the Greek Fathers, I had no idea that its use would cause such violent reactions, especially from ecclesiastical writers" (page 5). Elsewhere, he observes that St. Paul used the word *gnosis* "to specifically designate the inner knowledge of the Divine Mysteries" (page 6).

11. Analyzed from a different but related angle, the enneagram can be defined as a form of esotericism, as a mode of interior knowledge involving concepts such as correspondences, living nature, imagination and mediations, and the experience of transmutation. This notion was discussed at some length in our earlier book, *Dimensions of the Enneagram: Triad, Tradition, Transformation* (The Lion and the Bee, Marshall, Michigan, 2004), 2–8.

2

Introduction to the System

The act of cleansing must be conducted by one's own self, without any self-pity. The motivator of this act is . . . living zeal. It is both chopper and knife, which always works extremely well when it is sharpened by Grace and guided by its suggestions. It is ruthless when it establishes itself in the heart. It cuts, ignoring the cries of its victim. It is for this reason that the work goes on successfully, and soon achieves its purpose.
~ St. Theophan the Recluse

INTEREST IN THE ENNEAGRAM during the past several decades is something of a phenomenon, with numerous books written to expound it, and countless retreats, lectures and conferences devoted to its spread. While entire swaths of the population have never heard of it, tens of thousands of others have been exposed to it and favorably impressed by what it has to offer. Though interest in it ranges in intensity, it has clearly become an intriguing presence in many spiritual, religious, psychological and New Age circles.

Why is this? We could offer a number of answers, any one of which would be true as far as it goes. We might, for example, suggest that its unique combination of

- spirituality and psychology,
- theory and practice,
- modern insight and traditional wisdom,
- shrouded history and mysterious symbolism, and
- esoteric and gnostic elements

have given those who are prepared for such things a sort of "one-stop" revival of a significant part of the *philosophia perennis,* or "eternal philosophy." Its attraction stands, we believe, as a testament to the nature of spiritual and metaphysical intelligence, demonstrating the tendency of human beings—given half a chance—to revert to perennial principles and insights, despite pervasive materialist, positivist and progressive propaganda. Nature will out . . . supernature, too.

In brief, the enneagram expedites our escape from the "false self," from the ego-centered personality that is at the root of so much distress. It does so by exposing and slaying that self, by way of an esoteric technique well adapted to explore human interiority. In this technique, the spiritual and the material, the inward and the outward, are all brought into play, with unification of personality the goal; it is a holistic discipline. There is continuity with the Hermetic emblem, "As above, so below," and with Biblical symbolism, as well, wherein the "scroll of a book" has "writing on the front and on the back" (Ezekiel 2:9–10), on, that is, the exoteric and esoteric levels alike.

The discipline of the enneagram is a subtle means of entering the inner work that leads to transmutation. It outlines a method by which to explore one's soul (or psyche) in detail, with thoroughness and accuracy. It draws the soul and its unhappy traits through an elaborate sieve, identifying the compulsions and complexes that oppress us. Moreover, it lays bare the soul to Him "who searches our hearts" (Romans 8:27), to Him who cleanses and purges, uplifts and reconciles.

The word "enneagram" (pronounced ANY-a-gram) is based on the Greek words for nine, *ennea*, and figure, *grammos*. The word "enneatypes" refers to the nine basic patterns of personality. An enneatype is something like a person with a glandular disorder, who has overdeveloped some aspect or aspects of his or her potentials. Thus, enneatype One is capable of either excellent judgment or the most extreme judgmentalism; enneatype Five, the most brilliant ideation or the most extreme eccentricity; enneatype Eight, the greatest heroism or the most extreme aggressiveness, and so forth. These overdeveloped characteristics, then, nourish either the greatest virtues or the worst vices, or something in between. If they lead to excesses and deterioration, they need to be identified, understood, reined in, balanced, and, in the end, integrated into the total person.

The enneatypes and their basic traits are, in brief:

• *The Two*—Generous, nurturing, friendly, helpful, flattering, possessive, vainglorious, coercive, histrionic, manipulative and hysterical.
• *The Three*—Appealing, accomplished, efficient, industrious, narcissistic, competitive, image-conscious, shallow, deceitful, malicious, vengeful.
• *The Four*—Authentic, original, individualistic, artistic, sensitive, romantic, introverted, self-absorbed, alienated, depressive, self-destructive.
• *The Five*—Visionary, perceptive, dispassionate, analytical, self-sufficient, withdrawn, cynical, iconoclastic, eccentric, phobic and paranoid.
• *The Six*—Faithful, dutiful, affectionate, cooperative, vigilant, cautious, belligerent, insecure, suspicious, fearful and defiant.
• *The Seven*—Enthusiastic, multi-talented, cheerful, optimistic, acquisitive, uninhibited, hyperactive, moody, excessive, debauched and self-destructive.
• *The Eight*—Strong, bold, commanding, magnanimous, independent, dominating, boastful, ruthless, reckless, vengeful and violent.
• *The Nine*—Accepting, serene, balanced, supportive, complacent, disengaged, resigned, stubborn, undeveloped, neglectful and ineffectual.
• *The One*—Principled, moral, conscientious, fair, orderly, impersonal, rigid, fussy, intolerant, self-righteous and punitive.

The enneagram consists of both a symbol (**see diagram 1**) and a body of knowledge. The symbol consists of a circle enclosing both an equilateral triangle and an irregular hexagram, while the body of knowledge explains the processes mapped upon the symbol. The symbol's geometric figures are arranged to produce nine equidistant points on the circumference, each point representing a personality type.

In doing its work, the enneagram harnesses symbolic imagination, an essential aspect of its effectiveness. This is important because symbols devolve from a higher sphere, a sphere opaque to ordinary reason and unable to be distilled into abstract concepts. In

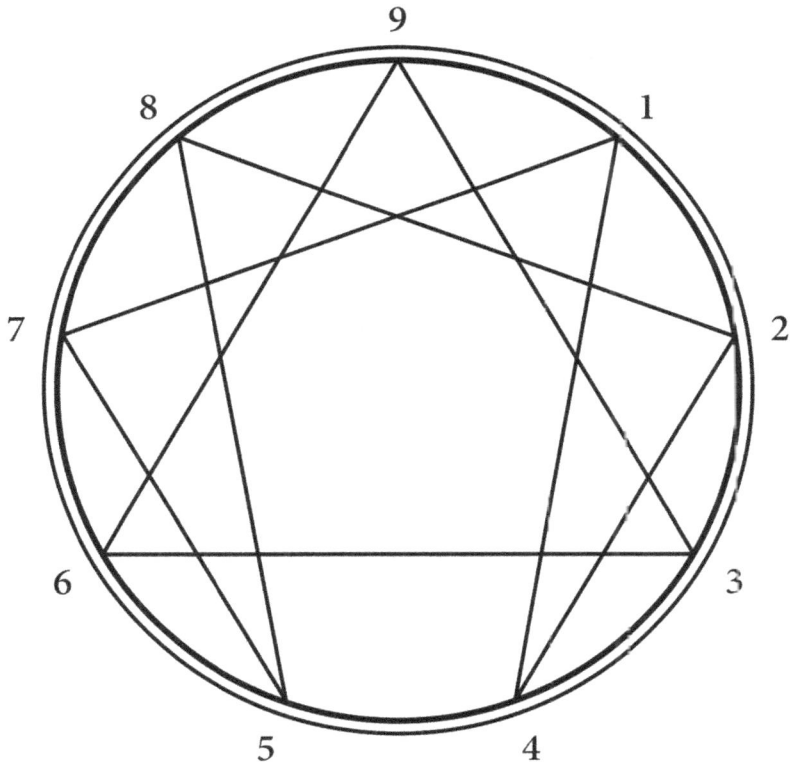

1. The Enneagram

spite of this—or because of it—they are capable of reaching the deepest levels of the self. By symbolic means, the enneagram helps to tame the turbulent sea of the ego, and the conscious and unconscious forces that feed it.

As a symbol, the enneagram effects its "magic" through internal communication, through wordless messages evoking the inner structure of the psyche and its contents, as well as the transcendent realities upon which it touches. According to the Russian esotericist, G.I. Gurdjieff, who introduced the symbol to Europe from the Near East early in the twentieth century, the equilateral triangle evokes the presence of "higher forces," the six-sided figure evokes the human person, and the circle evokes unity, wholeness and oneness.

That the hexagram is open at the base speaks to a link with both the lunar cycle—the phases of the moon—and the Pythagorean and Christian teaching of Evagrius Ponticus, a "desert father" of the fourth century who will be discussed at some length below. Correspondence between the lunar cycle and the "gap" at the base of the hexagram is suggested by researchers Virginia Wiltse and Helen Palmer.[1] In their insightful paper, they employ a chart illustrating the twenty-seven days in which the moon is visible and the single day (at the base) when it is invisible. The blank interval, representing the invisible phase of the moon, is shown to correspond to the gap at the base of the enneagram. Moreover, the twenty-seven visible phases accommodate the enneagram's twenty-seven subtypes (based on enneatype, wings and instinctual variants).

Quite independently of these reflections, a comparable lunar chart appears in the 1925 book, *A Vision,* by the poet and esotericist William Butler Yeats. In this curious volume, the author employs a personality typology based on twenty-*eight* phases of the moon, and, apropos of the preceding paragraph, includes a gap at the base of the chart to represent the day when the moon is dark. Despite its obscurity, the system indicates an inspiration not dissimilar to the

---

1. In a revised article entitled "Hidden in Plain Site: Observations on the Origins of the Enneagram," in the 2011 edition of the International Enneagram Association's *Enneagram Journal.*

sort that influenced Evagrius, and finds a certain cachet in the fact
that it was taken up by a first-class talent and a deep thinker, a man
well acquainted with "sacred science."

In its dynamic symbolism, the enneagram represents the disintegration and integration of the personality. Disintegration is represented by the sequences 1-4-2-8-5-7-1 and 9-6-3-9 and integration by
the reverse sequences, 1-7-5-8-2-4-1 and 9-3-6-9. The first sequence,
on the hexagram, results from dividing one by seven (which yields
.142857 into infinity and contains no multiples of three) while the
second sequence, the 9, 6 and 3 on the triangle, involves dividing
one by three (or one by six, or one by nine), which results in endless
repetition (one divided by three, for example, yields 0.333333...).

The enneagram has links to the Babylonians, Pythagoreans, Neo-
Platonists and others. As observed, there is a special link to Evagrius
Ponticus, whose teaching is marked by themes, vocabulary and
insights that clearly resonate with it. His influence can be seen not
only in lunar cycles and psychological types but in "essence," passions, and levels of integration and disintegration.

In his *Praktikos*, he taught there were eight dynamic and interre-
lated *logismoi* or "passionate thoughts." These eight, correlative to
all but one of the enneagram types, are pride (type two), vainglory
(three), sadness (four), avarice (five), gluttony (seven), impurity
(eight), acedia (nine) and anger (one). These passions are equivalent to the enneatypes, absent Type Six. John Cassian, a fifth century
monk, also taught the eight passions (as did others), while Gregory
the Great regularized all but one of them as the Seven Capital Sins.

According to Evagrius, the psyche was the seat of the passions,
above whose turbulence could be found "essential contemplation."
This higher realm of "essence" could be reached in stages, as one
climbed the "cosmic ladder" of virtue, by purification and prayer. To
him, as to Clement of Alexandria before him, the passions were to
be transmuted into deep, abiding calm: into *apatheia*. This Greek
word (the root of "apathy") meant release from the discord of
the passions, hence freedom from conflicts preventing one from
developing a balanced personality, and attainment of essential contemplation. Evagrius also taught the "application of opposites," a
principle not unlike the enneagram theory of integration and disin-

tegration, with its working for or against the "arrows," as will be explained. This principle dominates his *Antirrheticos* and appears elsewhere in his writings as well.

Evagrius's influence had a geographical sway to it. It was widespread in both Syrian and Armenian churches and, consequently, influential in a crossroads area of the world. Moreover, his manuals became sources of the ascetico-mystical way of Persian monasticism. Babia the Great, abbot of the monastery of Mt. Isla, "introduced Evagrius's works so successfully into Persia that they continued to be [influential] even after the Moslem conquest, and have decisively influenced the development of the spirituality of the Persian Sufis."[2]

Another link is Raymond Lull, the Franciscan mystic and missionary (1235?–1315), whose voluminous works contain a variety of enneagram drawings. Though clearly enneagrams, these are far more complex than the symbol used today. It is noteworthy, however, that he cataloged nine virtues and nine vices.[3]

Yet another link is found in the frontispiece of the *Arithmologia* of the Jesuit polymath, Athanasius Kircher, published in Rome in 1665. The book is a compendium of magical formulas, arcane symbols, talismans, number games and Kabbalistic diagrams. Again, as with Lull, the enneagram in the frontispiece—consisting of three equilateral triangles—differs from the one used in today's typology.

In the anti-traditional climate in which we find ourselves, a system and symbol like the enneagram of personality types stands out boldly. It marries symbol and detailed body of knowledge; it enlists both imagination and reason. It mystifies and intrigues, resonates and attracts, drawing us into hitherto unexplored realms, giving birth to deep understandings of the inner life. In this, it carries the sort of transmuting power that Giordano Bruno (1548–1600) attributed to a variety of mandala-type symbols. Though Bruno, the

---

2. Evagrius Ponticus: *The Praktikos* and *Chapters on Prayer,* translated with notes and introduction by John Eudes Bamberger, OCSO (Cistercian Publications, Kalamazoo, Michigan, 1981), li.

3. Anthony Bonner and Eve Bonner, editor and translator, *Doctor Illuminatus: A Ramon Lull Reader* (Princeton University Press, 1993), 333–334.

Renaissance philosopher, drew and meditated upon many such symbols, he possessed an abiding interest in one in particular.[4]

The enneagram has a similar effect on those who take it seriously.

A Word About Wings

"Wings" are the types on either side of a person's basic enneatype, and need to be addressed, if only briefly.

For example, if a person is a Five, he or she will have either a Four or a Six wing. The wing will color that person's "Fiveness." Thus a Five with a Four wing will manifest certain characteristics of the Four (some tendency to emotionalism or artistic temperament, perhaps) while a Five with a Six wing will manifest certain characteristics of the Six (a sense of team spirit or insecurity).

The concept of wings is an important one as it sheds light on the types and their complexities. It should be noted that the subject has been discussed at length in several places, most thoroughly in *Personality Types, Using the Enneagram for Self Discovery,* by Don Richard Riso and Russ Hudson, which we recommend.

Although there is no need to discuss the theory of wings in great detail here, readers unfamiliar with the enneagram might wish to have some additional idea of how the concept is applied to the various enneatypes. Thus the types and their wings, in brief compass, appear as follows:

---

4. Marie-Louise Von Franz, *Alchemical Active Imagination* (Shambala, Boston, Mass., 1997), 38. "Bruno pointed out," she writes, "that if one meditated on this chemically real mandala for years, one unified one's own inner personality and saved one's soul from extraverted distractions and dissociation." Our investigations have failed to identify the symbol in question. It is of interest, however, that Bruno was a devotee of the work of Raymond Lull. Hence, the following comments by Dorothea Waley Singer are intriguing also: "Bruno expounds an elaborate myth. . . . Progress, we are told, is not direct from one to another form. Rather—by an image reminiscent of the writings of Raymond Lull—change may be likened to motion around a wheel, so that each in turn is illuminated by the object in which converge the trinity of perfections. . . . Thus is revealed to us the ultimate harmony of the whole, the true meaning of the nine spheres. We see that the beginning of one is the end of another." (*Giordano Bruno: His Life and Thought* [Henry Schumann, New York, 1950], 131). One can hardly assume that the "chemically real" mandala mentioned by Von Franz is in fact an enneagram, yet the quoted portions from Singer's work are suggestive of a sensibility clearly responsive to similar structures and dynamics.

The Two with a One wing experiences conflict between the emotional, interpersonal and melodramatic traits of the Two and the rational, impersonal and self-controlled traits of the One. The subtype has a strong conscience (compliments of the One) that militates against the urge to act always according to emotional needs. There are conflicts between "head" and "heart." By contrast, the traits of the Two and those of the Three-wing tend to reinforce each other, as both types relate easily to people.

The Three with a Two wing has highly developed interpersonal skills, as the traits of the Three and the Two wing complement each other. The subtype tends to be at the center of attention and very charming. By contrast, the traits of the Three and the Four wing are often in conflict. The interpersonal Three is influenced by the withdrawing Four, resulting in a subtype that looks quite different— and more private—than the stereotypically outgoing and social Three.

The Four with a Three wing exhibits a measure of inner conflict, as the principal type works to harmonize the search for inner authenticity with the Three's easy ability to project an image popular with others. By contrast, the traits of Fours and Fives are congenial, with the Five adding intellectual depth.

The Five with a Four wing faces considerable conflict, as the cerebral, stand-offish Five cannot always deal comfortably with the emotionalism of the Four. The subtype is a rich one, however, combining artistic as well as intellectual gifts. By contrast, the traits of the Five and a Six wing complement each other but not always in happy ways. The distrustfulness of both types diminishes their interpersonal relations.

The Six with a Five wing evinces a conflict of traits, as the principal type is characterized by dependency on others while the Five is detached. By contrast, the traits of the Six harmonize with those of a Seven wing. In this instance, there is a tendency for the dutiful Six to be more extroverted and sociable.

The Seven with a Six wing experiences a measure of disharmony, inasmuch as the Six is oriented towards others while Sevens are oriented towards things and experiences. Sevens take care of their own needs. The Seven with an Eight wing, a "real presence in the room," is a personality of which others take notice. The traits of both are aggressive, and the subtype is doubly aggressive.

The Eight with a Seven wing is, again—owing to the resonance of the two types—a very aggressive subtype. In fact, owing to the dominance of the Eight, this is the *most* aggressive and *most* egocentric of the subtypes. By contrast, there is some conflict between the traits of an Eight and those of a Nine wing. Here, the wing curbs the aggressive stance and makes the subtype more interested in other people.

The Nine with an Eight wing exhibits a measure of conflict, as the traits of the Nine tend towards passivity and good relations with others, while the Eight wing adds a degree of strong self-assertion. By contrast, the traits of the Nine and those of a One wing are mostly harmonious. Here both types repress their emotions but for different reasons, the Nine to maintain peace and the One to maintain self-control.

The One with a Nine wing enjoys a harmony of traits, as each component of the subtype distances itself from the environment, creating a somewhat cool and detached personality. There is, on the other hand, a measure of conflict in a One with a Two wing. The controlled, rational One becomes warmer and more involved with others, more of a "people person."

An additional refinement of the enneagram system, the "levels of development," is an original teaching of Don Riso's that uses a nine-level continuum within each type to better understand the movements from healthy to average to unhealthy states, then back again.

Yet another refinement is the theory of instinctual subtypes, these being the self-preservation, social and sexual instincts. These, too (first taught by Oscar Ichazo, a seminal figure in development of what has become the enneagram of personality types), have been elaborated elsewhere, as in the Riso-Hudson book already mentioned, wherein they are called "instinctual variants." In brief, the self-preservation subtype is preoccupied with survival needs such as food, money, shelter, health and comfort; the social subtype, with group interactions, including desire for attention, recognition, success, appreciation, fame, and "being in the know;" the sexual subtype, with a desire for intense experience, be it a sexual encounter, a riveting conversation, or the sharing of an intimate secret.

3

Essence and Psyche

The essence of intelligence can only be union, namely synthesis, not analysis . . . contemplation, not discrimination.

~ Frithjof Schuon

SELF-REMEMBERING is the attempt to be aware of who we are. It is the attempt to be aware that we are double in ourselves; that two selves within us strive. The division is between psyche (soul) and essence (spirit); self-remembering attends to both as if our lives depended on it—which they do. Unification occurs by way of spiritual transmutation, by way, that is, of integration of the soul's scattered elements.[1]

Unification is accomplished by combined action of psyche, essence, divine Essence, and human-divine intellect, the last of which serves as conduit between the first three. By bringing psyche and essence into harmony, the rational, emotional and volitional faculties of the former are not "swallowed up" in essence without remainder but brought to their fullest and most balanced expression.

It may be said with confidence that anyone familiar with the enneagram is familiar with the concept of essence, though the importance attached to it varies from one person to the next. In the minds of some, it is a vague state of being, to which little meaning is

---

1. Robert Bolton observes that not all integrated—that is, authentic—persons are healthy. Authenticity by itself, he says, "is not enough to guarantee that one will be in the truth . . . because the authentic integration of the three 'spheres' of soul-life can still be pathological, varying from the mildly insane to the positively evil. Adolph Hitler is a modern prototype of the evil authentic man: his integration of idea-emotion-action was as sound as it could be in any saint." (*Self and Spirit* [Sophia Perennis, Hillsdale, New York, 2005], 63).

attached; merely a piece of furniture that came with the house. To others, it *remains* more or less a vague state of being, yet something to be—somehow—aspired after. To others still, it commands great interest; indeed, it is a consuming interest, representing the apex of psycho-spiritual exertions. To such as these, attainment of essence is the point of it all. This book falls largely into the latter category— ultimately, it *is* the point of it all—though not initially at the expense of the psychological domain. Nor, we must add, at the expense of the corporeal domain. For we are tripartite, constituted of essence (spirit), psyche (soul) and corpus (body) (**see diagram 2**).

To make sure our terms are clear before we proceed, we define essence as the spiritual part of us, as that aspect of our being that transcends personality, as the *essential self* or ground of our being, as the "image" of God residing in our inmost core. Although the Spirit of God and the human spirit are distinguished (Romans 8: 16), God's Spirit is able to infuse Himself into the receptive human spirit. As for the psyche, it is the soul of a man, the thinking, feeling and willing entity that mediates spirit and body; it is the internal consciousness of which personality is the outer expression.

If essence and psyche are not carefully distinguished, they tend to be conflated into ego (the conscious "I" or self of the psyche), reducing us to one-dimensional entities, dependant on reason, sentiment and volition alone, with no link to the transcendent domain. This is a common error at the present time, but not without a great deal of precedent. For as the Western understanding passed by degrees from the traditional to the modern view, the concept of essence was dropped and the tripartite concept itself reduced to a bipartite one. Spirit and soul (essence and psyche) became an indivisible "spirit-soul" without distinction, a "ghost in the machine" and, in time, all but vanished, leaving only the machine, or body, behind.

 This machine does, to be sure, have within it an animating principle that functions as an ego, as noted above. Despite the elimination of essence, contemporary thought has retained psyche. Thus, "psychology" is a science and a therapy, addressed to the variable and subjective psyche within. It is this remnant self that is "adjusted" by the skillful therapist; this entity whose unsteady and discordant elements are harmonized—or so it is hoped—in relation

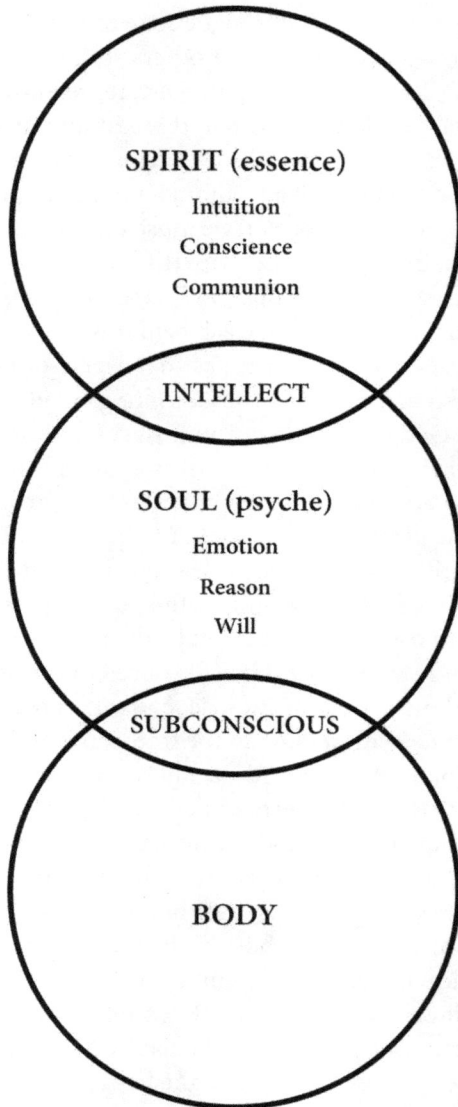

SPIRIT (essence)

Intuition

Conscience

Communion

INTELLECT

SOUL (psyche)

Emotion

Reason

Will

SUBCONSCIOUS

BODY

2. The Triadic Anthropology of the Enneagram

to one another and to the surrounding milieu. In all of this, essence is nowhere to be found.

More than any other individual, it was René Descartes who was responsible for the shift from a tripartite to a bipartite anthropology. His duality consisted of a purely mental soul (or mind) on the one hand, and a purely mechanical material world, on the other. Spirit was eliminated. The *substance* of the soul, its created identity, was eliminated as well, making way for later denials that a thinker exists at all, that an actual, individual entity really thinks the thoughts that are being thought. In these latter views, the mind is less a mind than the mere sum of its thoughts; less an existential entity than a process; less a sentient being than a stream of consciousness. The lights are on . . . but no one is home!

Descartes also neglected the faculty of "intellect," the source of intellectual intuition and the conduit between spiritual and psychical domains. Yet "activation" of this dormant faculty is the very thing that heals the rupture that agitates the soul. To the Scholastics, intellect (*intellectus*) possessed direct knowledge of principles, unlike the rational mind (*ratio*), which reasoned discursively, step by step. This faculty was for centuries known as the "active" or "agent" intellect, derived from Aristotle and handed down by Muslim and Jewish scholars. Through this agency, human beings possessed a fixed and stable set of concepts, a unified and accurate intuition of universals; in brief, an access to the eternal ideas that are the immutable reasons behind things. Intellect was seated "in the Sanctuary of [man's] personal Temple,"[2] linked to a supra-individual light and knowledge.

2. Antoine Faivre, quoting Martines de Pasqually (in *Access to Western Esotericism* [State University of New York Press, Albany, 1994], 158). Pasqually, founder of the *Elus Cohens*, employed a symbolism illustrative of the tripartite schema found in various religions, traditional symbolism, esotericism generally, fraternal and secret societies, and, of course, the enneagram. According to Faivre, he taught "that the Universal Temple, Nature, is divided into three parts: terrestrial, celestial, and supracelestial. Likewise, Solomon's Temple had three parts: the Porch, the Inner Temple and the Sanctuary. Similarly the human body has belly, chest, and head [all of which parallels the enneagram's tripartite division into physical, psychical and essential faculties]. In each case the three parts are inseparable." (157–158).

With these things in mind, it is clear that "essence" must be retained as a significant concept in any discussion of the enneagram. In essence one finds the core of the person, the transcendent principle. No amount of integration on the psychical level alone can replace integration of psyche into essence, soul into spirit, becoming into Being. Psyche is veil and instrument of the spiritual self, linked by intellect to essence. Only by integration into essence does it come fully into its own.

4

The Nine Enneatypes

Two: the Helper

"The quality of mercy is not strain'd.
It droppeth as the gentle rain from heaven."
∼ Shakespeare

THE TWO, THE HELPER, is on the "wing" of the Triad of emotion. Obedient to the conscience and its demand to help others, this type (when healthy) embodies empathy, compassion
and warm-heartedness. There is a nurturing quality; they drip with
"the milk of human kindness." They are ready to stand in the place
of Christ and say to others, "Come to me all you who are weary and
burdened, and I will give you rest" (Matthew 11:28).

Broadly speaking, in the Bible, two affirms *difference;* it points to
the *other* for good or ill. "The *two* may be, though different in character, yet one as to testimony and friendship . . . help and deliverance."[1] This speaks well of the type, but there is another side.
"Where man is concerned, this number testifies of his fall, for it
more often denotes that difference which implies *opposition, enmity,*
and *oppression.*"[2]

Veiled enmity or no, type Two wishes to be a provider of "help
and deliverance." There is in this wish an element of pride that can
be the downfall of the type. There is, in this wish, an impulse for
Twos to run themselves ragged in the attempt to do good deeds.

---

1. E. W. Bullinger, *Number in Scripture* (Kregel Publications, Grand Rapids,
Mich., 1967), 92.
2. Ibid.

After all, as they see it, the world is desperate to be healed. It is a place of neediness, pain and affliction. In response, they are compelled to be active: generous souls rushing to the rescue, bringing gifts of empathy and relief ("I feel your pain"). They dispense healing, compassion and good will.

The Two is a "heart type," an outgoing feeling type who not only loves but who wishes to be loved in turn. As a result of the latter, Helpers are prone to inflate their self-worth, with a desire for attention. To this end, they may play a variety of roles, including that of the martyr, ready and willing to sacrifice for others. Yet despite a sense of their own virtue, they are capable of belittling others, instilling guilt in them, and using them for their own purposes. Moreover, in carrying out their personal projects, they can be showy, "gushy," overly intimate and possessive. Yet they deny their ulterior motives, especially their anger and bitterness when others do not respond the way they want them to.

Elements of the Two can be seen in Karen Horney's "self-effacing solution," in which she observes that the subject's "idealized image of himself primarily is a composite of 'lovable' qualities, such as unselfishness, goodness, generosity, humility, saintliness, nobility, sympathy. Helplessness, suffering, and martyrdom are also secondarily glorified . . . a premium is also placed on feelings—feelings of joy or suffering, feelings not only for individual people but for humanity. . . . To have deep feelings is part of his image."[3]

The capital sin of Twos is pride. In their desire to be loved and admired for their good deeds and self-sacrifice, they actually put themselves and not others at the center of interest. Religious belief can reinforce this tendency, as Twos come to see themselves as saints, set apart for special service—for all the world to see. God is hardly needed, or so it seems, when a Two is on the scene.

Hence, it is a tendency of Helpers to see themselves as superior to ordinary mortals. Unconsciously, as prideful people, they see themselves as source and center of their own lives and of the lives of

---

3. *Neurosis and Human Growth: The Struggle Toward Self-Realization* (W.W. Norton and Company, Inc., New York, 1991), 222–23.

others. They want to give as only God can give, and to be loved for doing so. Yet pride licenses them to commit not only good deeds but bad ones also; it allows bad behavior for a perceived benevolent end, all the while fixing attention on their own importance.

Not that Twos are more blameworthy than other types, for pride as such feeds the root temptation, or capital sin, of each of them. For each type seeks to substitute its particular attempt to achieve autonomy, based on perfection (the One), success (the Three), self-reliance (the Eight), and so forth, in place of submission to God. Pride is self-worship. The Two exemplifies it according to the mode described in this chapter, but its variation on self-worship, though labeled "pride," is no more symptomatic of vainglory than the root sins of the other types.

As already intimated, Helpers can develop many aspects of themselves in the attempt to meet the needs of others. This can be a good thing if centered in a healthy sense of self, as in St. Paul's becoming "all things to all men" in an effort to rescue the lost. When this tendency arises from a fragmented self out of touch with its own deeper motives and potentials, it can sow mischief and misunderstanding instead of harmony and empathy.

Truth be told, Twos are as needy as anyone else. Unlike other types, however, they suppress their own needs and project them onto others. In doing so, in, that is, ascribing to others the feelings, thoughts, or attitudes present in themselves, they become convinced that others need their help. Sometimes "help" is accepted, though in fact it may be unhelpful or unnecessary. In such cases, it may even feed the recipient's weaknesses, promoting co-dependence.

Twos tend to approach others emotionally, putting personal considerations above tact or convention, human need above "the rules." They can become devoted, empathetic friends and helpers, and, at their best, display a generosity and a loyalty that merits the highest praise. Yet, when less than healthy, they can be hovering and meddlesome, invasive of others' personal space, given to swooping down on their chosen prey. They may wish to chat at awkward times, or exaggerate their emotions to excite the attention of others.

As feeling types, they are keenly aware of others' feelings towards them, and of their feelings towards others. Often affected and theatrical, they are skilled in the arts of flattery. Attentive and eager to please, they can become effusive and doting. Here as elsewhere, they allow their feelings the upper hand, even as reason is minimized. "Nothing disturbs feeling so much as thinking. It is therefore understandable that in this [extroverted feeling] type thinking will be kept in abeyance as much as possible."[4] Indeed, thinking becomes an "appendage" to feeling.[5] As a result, some Twos develop neither a realistic view of others nor a sober view of themselves.

The speech of Twos is frequently vague. ("He's *such* a wonderful person.") It is speech designed to please, rather than to communicate substance. It tends to be "lip labor" (in the phrase of Jacob Boehme) and little else. Moreover, when speaking such empty words, Twos are indirectly seeking the attention, praise and assurance of others. They are, in fact, often engrossed in themselves and barely able to hear what others are saying. It is the mood, the "feel" of the conversation that has the priority.

Often sweet or "precious," Twos—especially females—can be seductive verbally and physically, exhibiting an allure that draws others. They may share intimacies, dropping comments about their private lives, as a means to their ends. There is a desire for sexual attention as a sign of approval, an erotic invitation that seeks to affirm one's self worth. In this, the Two, as elsewhere, can become invasive and even smothering, sometimes putting off rather than attracting others. At such times, they become possessive, manipulating others and drawing them away from friends and acquaintances. The person thus singled out is jealously guarded, for the Two aspires to be the principal influence. Other persons are to remain at arm's length.

In being possessive, Helpers can be domineering, demanding and coercive as well; they can be impatient, quick with advice, eager to direct the lives of others—all in the name of love. Again, in all of this, they "need to be needed;" they need to be loved for the many things they do. As self-appointed martyrs, they feel entitled to the gratitude of others and they will put "in their place" anyone who

---

4. C.G. Jung, *Psychological Types* (Princeton University Press, Princeton, NJ, 1971), 357.
5. Ibid.

opposes their attempts to help. ("If you had listened to my advice, everything would have worked out okay.")

Not surprisingly, Helpers can be condescending in an obvious and off-putting way. This tendency indicates an assumed superiority on the part of the Two, which fits the profile of the self-proclaimed saint. Clearly, this attitude demonstrates moral one-upmanship, not concern for the welfare of the other.

When discouraged, Twos may seek the love they think they're due by becoming hypochondriacs, suffering a "nervous breakdown" or developing emotionally based illnesses. This is not wholly unexpected in a "feeling" type like the Two. Angry because their needs (as they define them) have not been met, hurt because others have not responded "as they should" to their reputed benevolence, and lacking ability to obtain the help they truly need, Twos may turn their aggressions inward and make themselves sick. Of course, others will get the blame.

François Fénelon, the epistolary Archbishop of Cambrais, addressed with keen insight a correspondent who clearly demonstrates type Two characteristics:

You have spent all your life in the belief that you are wholly devoted to others, and never self-seeking. Nothing so feeds self-conceit as this sort of internal testimony that one is quite free from self-love, and always generously devoted to one's neighbors. But all this devotion that seems to be for others is really for yourself. Your self-love reaches to the point of perpetual self-congratulation that you are free from it; all your sensitiveness is lest you might not be fully satisfied with self; this is at the root of all your scruples. It is the "I" which makes you so keen and sensitive. You want God as well as man to be always satisfied with you, and you want to be satisfied with yourself in all your dealings with God.

Besides, you are not accustomed to be contented with a simple good will—your self-love wants a lively emotion, a reassuring pleasure, some kind of charm or excitement. You are too much used to be guided by imagination and to suppose that your mind and will are inactive, unless you are conscious of their workings.

And thus you are dependent upon a kind of excitement similar to that which the passions arouse, or theatrical representations .... It is mere self-love to be inconsolable at seeing one's own imperfections; but to stand face to face with them, neither flattering nor tolerating them, seeking to correct oneself without becoming pettish—this is to desire what is good for its own sake and for God's.[6]

Virtually every major shortcoming of type Two—and not a few minor ones, as well—can be found in this perceptive letter. The letter may seem overly critical, as might so much else in this chapter, but most persons wear blinders in regard to their faults, not their virtues. Thus, the enneagram must unmask and expose; only then can it build up. Other types will receive equally penetrating scrutiny, as will become clear in the pages ahead.

The disintegrating Helper, then, adrift in unhappy straits, is only half of the picture. The other half represents a person truly unselfish toward others. The better angels of the type are found in those who are solicitous, cooperative, considerate, amiable, delightful, charming—all the things a good and helpful person should be. Such exemplars, devoted to the real welfare of those around them, are responsive, attentive, and generous to a fault. They find it more blessed to give than to receive.

In their concern for others, healthy Twos provide the all-around support that individuals need at various stages of their lives, helping them to achieve their proper ends. In doing so, they offer advice in a non-judgmental and empathic manner. Warmhearted and outgoing, they do right by both God and their fellows, "for he who loves his fellow man has fulfilled the law" (Romans 13:8).

They also learn to be "helpers" to themselves, to take into account their legitimate needs, and to see the pride involved in refusing to do so. For the opposite of pride is not humility so much as it is self-respect; respect of the person that God has created and called, of the one who is saint and sinner, and of the one who needs to admit his

6. Aldous Huxley, *The Perennial Philosophy* (Harper & Row Publishers, Inc., New York, 1944), 253–54.

or her limitations as a flawed and finite being. Helpers at this level have learned the true meaning of caring and, yes, of humility, and are living out these virtues for the good of all—themselves included.

In the Bible, Mary the mother of Jesus appears to be a Two. Of course, the Bible nowhere gives anything like a full account of an individual's personality; rather, one catches glimpses of various figures and the actions in which they engage. There are exceptions, including the portraits of Jesus, Peter, and David. For example, the personality of Jesus can be seen in much detail and from many angles in the Gospels. In the case of Peter, the traits of an impetuous but big-hearted man are clearly evident. As to David, not only does a detailed portrait emerge from the dramatic events of his life, but he can be seen "from the inside" in the Psalms that are credited to him.

In its presentation of the archaic figures who peopled the Mediterranean world and the Near East two, three and four-thousand years ago, the Bible carries within itself a sort of "archetypal" aspect in relation to psychological type, a sort of original pattern or first form that finds itself repeated down through the ages. Thus patterns of human personality can be discerned in the sacred writings, if not often in great detail at least in broad strokes. These early figures— especially in the early books—were "prototypes" of what one sees today.

Mary the mother of Jesus appears to have been a dedicated Helper, a healthy Two. Her devoted service was rendered to God and to her son. A humble maiden, she submitted to God and she praised God for the honors bestowed upon her. She kept the mysteries made known to her "hidden in her heart," where she pondered them. Her singular service in the great scheme of salvation history, acquitted with grace and humility, extended even to a faithful recollection of certain of the marvelous facts of the salvation story, as she is the most likely source of the infancy narratives recorded years after the event.

Despite her virtues and holy service, Mary's humanness is evident in a number of passages. Though surrounded by signs of the supernatural, she seemed at times to be unaware of her son's mission and his single-minded dedication to that mission. When she and Joseph found their twelve-year-old son in the temple courts after he had been missing several days—found him discoursing on an equal footing with the teachers of religion—they did not grasp the meaning of his statement that he "had to be in [his] Father's house." Nor did she understand, at the wedding in Cana, that her son's hour had not yet come when she asked him to rescue a party running short of wine. Again, she and the brothers of Jesus on more than one occasion came to remove him after others had claimed he was "beside himself" and possessed by Beelzebub.

Jesus was himself a Helper (and infinitely more than a Helper, of course), readily available throughout his life to teach and heal and feed the crowds who came to him. At the same time, this "man for others" was not opposed to taking time for himself, time to recollect what had occurred in his mission and to plan for what lay ahead, time to be alone with the Father. "Very early in the morning, while it was still dark, Jesus got up, left the house and went off to a solitary place, where he prayed" (Mark 1:35). Jesus needed to be alone with the Father, to rest and reflect and be refreshed. The Two needs to do the same. There are times—more times than the Two may be willing to admit—when God's will for His servants is to put their own needs first, to put rest and food and self-reflection—and even play— ahead of service to others.

Another temptation is the desire to draw attention to oneself. The Helper tends to do just this, as he or she relishes being noticed for doing good deeds. This is not the recommended attitude, according to the Sermon on the Mount, or to the whole tenor of traditional wisdom, for that matter. "So when you give to the needy, do not announce it with trumpets, as the hypocrites do in the synagogues and on the streets, to be honored by men. I tell you the truth, they have received their reward in full. But when you give to the needy, do not let your left hand know what your right hand is doing, so that your giving may be in secret. Then your Father, who sees what is done in secret, will reward you" (Matthew 6:1–4).

Likewise, Jesus warns of wrong motives in the prayer life and in the practice of fasting. In both cases, the temptation to parade one's virtues before others is firmly rebuked, and the believer is urged to practice his devotions with regard to God alone. Again, "Your Father, who sees what is done in secret, will reward you" (vss 6, 18).

As noted earlier, Twos can be careless in speech. A kind of rote flattery, superficial and deceitful, serves as a means of manipulating others. This is perilous to the soul of the Two and potentially harmful to those who are receptive to insincere praise. "Whoever flatters his neighbor is spreading a net for his feet" (Proverbs 29:5). The "neighbor" may take the flattery seriously, puffing himself up and thereby courting future disappointments.

Jesus takes the words a person speaks with utmost seriousness: "But I tell you that men will have to give account on the day of judgment for every careless word they have spoken. For by your words you will be acquitted, and by your words you will be condemned" (Matthew 12:36). A sobering thought, this, linking merely careless words with judgment. Straightforward honesty is the recommended course. "Let your 'Yes' be 'Yes,' and your 'No,' 'No'" (Matthew 5:37).

In swelling pride, Helpers view themselves as saviors of the world, called to shower good deeds on the helpless and the needy. They would be wise to curb their pride with the awareness that God is already at work, helping and sustaining and providing, even in the worst of circumstances. "Because of the LORD'S great love we are not consumed, for his compassions never fail. They are new every morning; great is [his] faithfulness" (Lamentations 3:22–23). The Lord is thus nearby, compassionate and involved, even in the darkest hour. Moreover, the Apostle Paul asserts, "He who did not spare his own Son, but gave him up for us all—how will he not also, along with him, graciously give us all things" (Romans 8:32). The Two's generous provision of help, virtuous in itself, is yet given in the context of God's grace in the unfolding of events.

In his life and doctrine, Jesus set the pattern for the healthy Two. In one instance, he contrasted the power-idolatry of the Roman world, with all of its pomp and hero worship, with the importance of service, an emphasis to which the Two should resonate: "You know that those who are regarded as rulers of the Gentiles lord it over them. . . . [May it not be] so with you. Instead, whoever wants to become great among you must be your servant, and whoever wants to be first must be slave of all. For even the Son of Man did not come to be served, but to serve, and to give his life as a ransom for many" (Mark 10:42–45).

Lastly, in the twelfth chapter of Romans, Paul offers further guidance to those—Twos especially—who are eager to be engaged in well doing. He touches on the humility, clear thinking and faith necessary to properly serve others. He touches, too, on the awareness of one's gifts and the need to exercise them in community: "For by the grace given to me, I say to every one of you: Do not think of yourself more highly than you ought, but rather think of yourself with sober judgment, in accordance with the measure of faith God has given you. . . . We have different gifts, according to the grace given us. If a man's gift is prophesying, let him use it in proportion to his faith. If it is serving, let him serve; if it is teaching, let him teach; if it is encouraging, let him encourage; if it is contributing to the needs of others, let him give generously; if it is leadership, let him govern diligently; if it is showing mercy, let him do it cheerfully" (vss 3, 6–8). The grace of God accounts for varied gifts, distributed as He wills among the personality types. The Helper's gifts, recognizable in the preceding passage, are most evident in serving, encouraging, showing mercy and giving generously.

Inclined to prideful airs, the Two would like to be all things to all people. This will not happen. Nonetheless, he or she embodies special gifts essential to helping those in need, gifts redounding to their credit. For a happy denouement awaits "those who by persistence in doing good seek glory, honor and immortality." For to them, "he will give eternal life" (Romans 2:7).

Three: the Achiever

No sooner does one realize with bitterness and sorrow the vileness of one's demoniac pretensions to excel—no sooner does one begin to loathe the dark spirit within—than the heart is led into the hitherto-unknown sphere of freedom.   ∼ Archimandrite Sophrony

LOCATED IN THE MIDDLE of the "heart center" (the Triad of Emotion), Achievers contend for success in the eyes of others. In the quest for worldly attainment, they display a charismatic quality that can inspire or manipulate, produce good or work evil.

Their capacity for good or evil is reflected in the number Three itself, which, on the one hand, "stands for the mortal condition, the disturbed, intermediate condition to which time and space belong,"[1] and, on the other hand, "for that which is *solid, real, substantial, complete,* and *entire*."[2] Thus the type is paradoxical: deceitful and divided in one aspect, honest and integrated in the other.

In their single-minded quest for success, Achievers indeed display both "disturbed" and healthy traits. Both come into play as they dream of themselves at the top of their field, as they visualize in detail each step on the path to eminence. In their unhealthy states, then, winning is the only thing, regardless of cost both to others and to themselves. In their healthier states, however, they "count the cost," applying a moral calculus to keep on the straight and narrow.

As they seek status and acceptance, Achievers gauge keenly the responses of others, aiming to measure up to the criteria of success defined by their culture or subculture. They are, to this end, driven, controlled, assertive, vigilant and self-reliant. They revolve around "me, myself and I." They are prone to exaggerate their abilities and accomplishments, while downplaying anything that might threaten their all-important self-esteem. They play a role; they wear a mask. Bit by bit, if not careful, their inner self vanishes from awareness until the outer shell alone remains.

The average to unhealthy Achiever has little use for the sobering and cautionary wisdom of Ecclesiastes: "I have seen all the things that are done under the sun; all of them are meaningless, a chasing after the wind" (1:4). Such is the Three's worst nightmare. To think that all the fame and glory after which he or she chases could in the end be "meaningless," to think it all a "vanity fair" of little or no enduring value, that is asking for more than a Three can accept. Threes are the last to comprehend the fleeting nature of fame; the last to realize their achievements will be forgotten; the last to fathom how little it all matters to others in the first place.

In pursuit of their dreams, Threes tend to activate their root sin,

---

1. Edmund D. Cohen, *C.G. Jung and the Scientific Attitude* (Philosophical Library, New York, 1975), 89.
2. Bullinger, *Number in Scripture*, 107.

deceit. With great smoothness and subtlety, they tell blatant lies or merely shade the truth, often without realizing it, so habitual does it become. They fool not only others by the things they say and the image they contrive but themselves as well, rendering their view of inner and outer reality subjective and distorted. In all of this, "truth" is an unconscious enemy, for it, like light, is therapeutic; it exposes and heals disease, be the disease interior or exterior. The disease of Threes is sloth of inner development, even as their outer development flourishes for all to see.

As observed, Threes crave success as defined by their social milieu. They judge themselves in terms of it, measuring personal worth by conformity to approved standards. In doing so, they devote themselves to the surface of life (to "all the vain things that charm me most"—Isaac Watts), fearing to look deeply into the meaning of existence. Of unhealthy Threes it can be said: "They exchanged the truth of God for a lie, and worshiped and served created things rather than the Creator" (Romans 1:5).

In pursuing their goals, Achievers are keenly aware they must attract attention. They will not, if they can help it, work patiently behind the scenes, like a dutiful Six. Rather, they present themselves front and center, employing every skill of self-promotion. Not surprisingly, they shine as show business personalities, politicians, sales representatives, or in other capacities in which personality, presentation and an air of confidence are paramount. "There is a star quality born of self-regard, self-respect, self certainty."[3]

Predictably, they are sophisticated and socially adept. They absorb the manners and nuances that please those whom they wish to impress. They flow with ease in the social current. The correct gesture, the apt phrase, come naturally to them. They are well groomed and often sexually attractive. They develop many relationships but few deep ones.

As indicated, Achievers are skilled talkers. Unlike verbally skilled Sevens, however, they use words to make a good impression and to

3. John M. Oldham, MD, and Lois B. Morris, addressing the "self-confident style" in their *Personality Self-Portrait, Why You Think, Work, Love, and Act the Way You Do* (Bantam Books, New York, 1991), 79.

further long-range goals. By contrast, the Seven is more interested in charming or seducing others for short-term purposes. In neither case is great attention paid to the deeper meanings of language or the ideas they express.

Of course, Achievers do not embody style over substance in every case. In some cases, they are the "genuine article," though made to look even better by skillful self-promotion. They tend, in fact, to be highly competent, qualified to meet challenges in their area of expertise. Just as they have a one-track mind for success, they are clear on the course to follow. They do not waste time or resources on side issues but take aim at the goal and pursue it aggressively. In doing so, they are clear-minded in their judgments, setting standards for themselves and others. Not surprisingly, they identify strongly with the enterprises to which they devote their time and energy. In addition, they come to their work prepared: advanced degrees, attendance at seminars, late hours at the office, whatever it takes to succeed. They work hard to shine before others.

When they are healthy and therefore balanced, Threes possess an inner dynamic that keeps them moving in a positive direction. They are infectious in their enthusiasm and readily attract others to their cause. As good team players (again, when healthy), they are skilled at motivating others to aspire after the same ends as they. They know the way to reach the goal is by building a team that works harmoniously. With their competent air, verbal talent and organizational acumen, they do just that. They bring success to those who labor with them, not to themselves only.

The words of Immanuel Kant point to the double-edged nature of the type: "Controlling the inclinations of other people in order to direct and manage them according to one's own intentions, almost amounts to being in possession of them as mere instruments of one's own will. It is not surprising, then, that striving after the faculty to have influence over others is a passion."[4]

---

4. *Anthropology from a Pragmatic Point of View,* translated by Victor Lyle Dowdell (Southern Illinois University Press, Carbondale and Edwardsville, Ill., 1996), 179.

The patriarch Jacob, son of Isaac and grandson of Abraham, appears to have been a Three. From his birth, he was in competition with Esau, his elder twin. Jacob, whose name means "heel-catcher" or "supplanter," held tight to his brother's heel at the moment of birth, and remained in pursuit of his brother's primacy in the years that followed. In this archetypal story of sibling rivalry, Jacob was encouraged in trickery by his mother, Rebecca, who may have acted as she did owing to a revelation from God (Genesis 25:23). She played the role that mothers or mother-substitutes often play in the lives of Threes, serving as the nurturing figure who provides essential mirroring for the child. Jacob was a "momma's boy," frequenting the tents and pursuing the settled routines of life while his rougher, heartier brother became a man of the outdoors and a skilled hunter. All the while, Jacob internalized his mother's favoritism.

Jacob first deceived his brother by exchanging a bowl of lentil stew for the latter's birthright. Later, with the connivance of his mother, he tricked his feckless father, too, and received the blessing that should have gone to Esau. Outraged, the elder brother determined to kill Jacob. Warned by his mother, Jacob fled to Harran to live with his uncle, Laban. On the way, he experienced his famous dream, in which he saw angels ascending and descending a stairway—or "ladder"—to heaven. In the dream, the Lord promised Jacob a vast territory and countless descendents. Success indeed! Deceiver though he was, he received a starring role in the divine plan.

In the years that followed, he came close to meeting his match in deceitfulness in the person of his uncle. The wily Laban tricked his nephew into first marrying Leah, the plainer of his two daughters, and then contrived to get fourteen years of work out of him as the price of marrying the beautiful Rachel, as well. Yet, in the course of his dealings with his uncle, Jacob's intelligence, industry and desire to succeed eventually worked their magic and the younger man surpassed the older in accumulating wealth.

At the Lord's prompting, Jacob at last returned to Canaan, accompanied by his family and flocks, slaves and servants. (In parting with her father, Rachel became a deceiver like her husband, stealing Laban's household gods and then hiding them.) As he neared his homeland, Jacob determined to mollify Esau by presenting him with generous gifts of livestock. Despite the gifts, Jacob's fear intensified when he was informed that his brother was approaching with four hundred men. In the event, Esau was anything but vengeful. Weeping, he kissed his errant brother, forgave him his misdeeds and welcomed him. A deferential Jacob parleyed with Esau and then took leave of his brother, indicating he would follow him home. Deceiving his brother yet again, he led his entourage in another direction.

A vital turning point in Jacob's life occurred on the eve of his reunion with Esau, when he "wrestled with God" on the banks of the River Jabbok. Jacob successfully sought a blessing but suffered a dislocated hip in the course of the struggle. Permanently lamed, this man of pride, self-reliance and cunning had at last met his match and yet, in yielding, received not only a blessing but a new name as well: Israel—"He who strives with God—and prevails.' Wounded, broken, flawed, but blessed, Jacob was equipped to fulfill his role in salvation history.[5]

Despite God's willingness to use Jacob in his plans, warnings against deceit, the root sin of the Three, are commonplace in the Bible. In the Ten Commandments, there is the admonition against "bearing false witness" and, in Leviticus 19:11, one reads, "Do not lie. Do not steal. Do not deceive one another." The Psalmist, too,

---

5. As in these and other Scriptures, the literal meaning frequently conceals an esoteric meaning, the exegesis of which is beyond the scope of this work. To be fair to the esoteric domain, however, a pair of examples shall be cited from the work of Samuel D. Fohr, beginning with the exchange of the lentil stew for Esau's birthright. "Now the birthright involves precedence, and there is no doubt that the world favors the lower tendencies [personified by Esau] and gives them precedence in human life. Everything is designed to foster and entrap people in these tendencies.... Esau's 'hunger' is merely a symbol of all the lower tendencies." Second, in regard to the dream, "The stairway connecting the sky and earth is the World Spirit or Axis connecting the Celestial and Terrestrial Paradises, and the angels symbolize the higher influences in their ascending and descending modes. Jacob has achieved the first stage on the spiritual journey in that he has traveled horizontally to his own true center. He must now travel vertically up the stairway, whose steps indicate higher states of existence, to the abode of God." See Samuel D. Fohr, *Adam & Eve: The Spiritual Symbolism of Genesis and Exodus* (Sophia Perennis, Hillsdale, New York, 2001), 142, 144.

speaks of falsehood: "How long will you love delusions and false gods?" (4:2). Proverbs puts it bluntly: "Better to be poor than a liar" (19:22). Here one finds an echo of Socrates in the *Apology:* "I have a sufficient witness to the truth of what I say—my poverty."[6]

As we have observed, Achievers are skilled at shading the truth and even lying as they strive after success, status and adulation. They find their ambitions more desirable than straight talk. After all, if corners must be cut, well, that's the way of the world. Yet . . . "Truth is one, and he who does the truth in the small thing is of the truth: he who will do it only in a great thing, who postpones the small thing near him to the great farther from him, is not of the truth." [7]In reaching for the top, Threes too often dismiss—consciously or unconsciously—the importance of the little unsung acts of honesty that anchor the moral life.

Jesus promised his followers they would know the truth and the truth would set them free. Hence, Achievers need to face the truth and to speak the truth, and, like Helpers, to let "their yea be yea and their nay be nay." They need to reorder their priorities, to become something more than "men of this world whose reward is in this life" (Psalm 17:14). They need to measure their lives against spiritual verities instead of the opinions of mankind.

As they answer the call to conversion, they need not abandon legitimate ambitions but need to pursue them in a different framework and with a changed motivation. The framework is the spiritual life, and the motivation is to use one's talents to glorify God not self. It may be true, as Samuel Johnson observed, that there are few ways in which men are more innocently employed than in "getting money," but such does not answer the soul's deepest needs.

Threes must choose whom they will serve. Jesus Christ addressed the point in a teaching as well known as it is neglected: "No one can serve two masters. Either he will hate the one and love the other, or

6. *The Dialogues of Plato,* 31, translated by Benjamin Jowett, in *Great Books of the Western World,* Robert Maynard Hutchins, editor in chief, (Encyclopaedia Britannica, Inc., Chicago, 1977), 207.

7. C.S. Lewis, *George MacDonald, An Anthology* (Macmillan Publishing Co., Inc., New York, 1969), 36.

he will be devoted to the one and despise the other. You cannot serve both God and money" (Matthew 6:24).

He who would walk the spiritual walk must part ways with the world (the world in the sense of sinful man, dedicated to unrighteousness and hostile to God and truth, not in the sense of the created order, with its multitude of human and natural goods). To be wedded to the fallen world is to be lost. "God wants us to walk in *obedience*—not victory. Obedience is oriented toward God: victory is oriented toward self. . . . This is not to say God doesn't want us to experience victory, but rather to emphasize that victory is a by-product of obedience."[8]

In a similar vein, the Apostle Paul upbraided the Corinthians, whose worldliness was the leaven of an otherwise Spirit-filled life. In 1 Corinthians, he urged "discernment of spirits;" he reminded them of their true benefactor: "We have not received the spirit of the world but the Spirit who is from God, that we may understand what God has freely given us" (2:12). Elsewhere, he urged the faithful to oppose self-seeking and to look after the welfare of others, clearly an unnatural inclination for unhealthy Achievers, not to mention the human race at large: "Do nothing out of selfish ambition or vain conceit, but in humility consider others better than yourselves. Each of you should look not only to your own interests, but also to the interests of others" (Philippians 2:3–4). The believer needs to be reminded that God does not choose mainly the VIPs of the world as his servants; often, he chooses the opposite: "Not many of you were wise by human standards; not many were influential, not many were of noble birth. But God chose the foolish things of the world to shame the wise; God chose the weak things of the world to shame the strong" (1 Corinthians 1:26–27).

Who comes first, God... or mammon? God, or personal achievement? God, or the applause of the crowd? In customary hyperbole, Jesus answered in the Sermon on the Mount:

Therefore I tell you, do not worry about your life, what you will eat or drink; or about your body, what you will wear. Is not life

8. Jerry Bridges, *The Pursuit of Holiness* (NavPress, Colorado Springs, 1989), 21.

more important than food, and the body more important than clothes? ... So do not worry, saying "What shall we eat?" or "What shall we drink?" or "What shall we wear?" For the pagans run after all these things, and your heavenly Father knows that you need them. But seek first his kingdom and his righteousness, and all these things will be given to you as well (Matthew 6:25, 31–33).

To follow this teaching, Threes must put personal ambition in second place. Yet for the unredeemed Three, this is unthinkable; it is to turn the world upside down. "For the message of the cross is foolishness to those who are perishing, but to us who are being saved it is the power of God" (1 Corinthians 1:18). To Threes (and not to Threes only), seeking first "his kingdom and his righteousness" is foolishness indeed.

Yet they need not fret, for in fact spiritual and natural goods normally correspond; the sober and sensible person, with good will towards the neighbor, generally reaps material as well as spiritual goods. Once a Three alters course, the "good things" of life—under normal circumstances—frequently follow in turn, provided he is not called to an ascetic life (which has its own compensations). One enters the kingdom "and all these things" are added. Clearly, a Three—again, under normal circumstances—should have healthy ambitions, enjoy a well-earned reputation, experience legitimate pleasures. For neither particular providence nor the effects of prayer can be limited to the spiritual life at the expense of the psycho-corporeal life. The Bible is replete with links between spiritual goods leading to natural goods, and spiritual evils leading to natural evils. To deny this, as an astute observer notes, is to embrace the "nine-tenths Deism of modern religious thought."[9]

Hence, the Bible does not encourage its hearers to wean themselves from natural life by suppressing their legitimate desires. Neither the Three nor any other type need fear such a teaching. "This barrier [between the Christian and the 'world'] is no surly contempt for life, no legalistic piety, it is the life which is life indeed, the gospel,

---

9. Robert Bolton, *Keys of Gnosis*, 98.

the person of Jesus Christ. . . . He wants to be the center, through him all things shall come to pass."[10] Creation is good: God made it. Rightly used, the things of creation (even though creation itself is "a good thing spoiled," in the words of C. S. Lewis) can and should be enjoyed.

Achievers need to rediscover the inner reality they have suppressed, owing to deceit toward themselves as well as others. During a life devoted to worldly ambition, the public persona may have swollen with success while the person behind the mask—the deepest and truest self—has shriveled. The Three has been heedless that "this world in its present form is passing away" (1 Corinthians 7:31). Instead, he or she has chosen the transitory image over the enduring principle.

Time and again, the teachings of Jesus point to the importance of the inner self, for example: "For out of the overflow of the heart the mouth speaks. The good man brings good things out of the good stored up in him, and the evil man brings evil things out of the evil stored up in him" (Matthew 12:34–35). Old Testament prophecy addresses the inner self in similar fashion: "'This is the covenant I will make with the house of Israel after that time,' declares the LORD. 'I will put my law in their minds and write it on their hearts'" (Jeremiah 31:33). Other traditions speak to the point, also: "He who aspires to [virtue] must resolve upon the good and attach himself strongly to it; he must apply himself to the study of himself, interrogate nature, examine all things carefully, meditate upon them and allow nothing to pass unfathomed."[11]

In addition, Achievers must learn that even good intentions, proper motivation, well-laid plans and great effort do not always lead to success. They have to make room for the possibility of failure without succumbing to despair, for God allows testing. Jesus warned his followers that persecutions would come, and it is undeniable that persons who stand up for principle can expect to incur

---

10. Dietrich Bonhoeffer, *The Cost of Discipleship* (Macmillan Publishing Co., Inc., New York, 1963), 106.

11. Fabre d'Olivet, *The Golden Verses of Pythagoras,* quoting Kong-Tse (Confucius), 202.

the wrath of the crowd at some point in their lives. "Blessed are you when people insult you, persecute you and falsely say all kinds of evil against you because of me. Rejoice and be glad, because great is your reward in heaven" (Matthew 5:11–12). Threes may be called to experience affliction, to take "time out" from seeking applause, to stand up for spiritual truth. If so, it is a singular moment, transmuting "poverty of spirit into heavenly humility."[12] Threes learn to "worship in spirit and in truth" (John 4:24), to forsake the idols of the market place and to put faith first, where it belongs.

In thus changing their outlook, they may experience an "immense elation and freedom, as the outlines of the confining selfhood melt down."[13] The reason is this: Threes, like other aggressive types, are in their average to unhealthy states almost totally unaware of their inner selves. Thus, in conversion or "metanoia," when the depths are stirred, change is sudden and emotionally charged. "These persons [the specific reference is to the 'somatotonic' of William Sheldon's famous typology] are so intensely extraverted as to be quite unaware of what is happening in the lower levels of their minds. If for any reason their attention comes to be turned inwards, the resulting self-knowledge, because of its novelty and strangeness, presents itself with the force and quality of a revelation and their metanoia, or change of mind, is sudden and thrilling."[14]

When the depths are stirred, then, change is dramatic; it is a "revelation," a welling up of the spirit within. Wayward Threes are "born again"... fitted to pursue the life of the kingdom, even as they have hitherto pursued the conceits of the world. They experience at last an abiding joy that displaces counterfeit goods and brings in their stead a message of fulfillment.

12. Benjamin B. Warfield, *Faith and Life* (The Banner of Truth Trust, 1990), 35.

13. William James, *The Varieties of Religious Experience* (Penguin Books, New York, 1986), 273.

14. Aldous Huxley, *The Perennial Philosophy*, 155–156.

The Nine Enneatypes

Four: the Artist

*We could say that the substance of the soul is the unconscious search for a
lost Paradise, which in reality is 'within you.'*
∼ Frithjof Schuon

THE "ARTIST," the creative individual who occupies the space of the
Four, bears in his person the symbolism of the number with which
he is identified. "The number *four* . . . follows the revelation of God
in the Trinity, namely *His creative works.* He is known by the things
that are seen."[1] Fours display their creative touch in a variety of
ways, be it in a work of art, a special style of dress, a fashionable
apartment or impeccable manners. They are "known by the things
that are seen."

Artists have a darker side as well, for in their unhealthy mode,
they are entangled in the poison vine of envy. They are envious
above all of the seeming normality of others, of the easy involve-
ment with day-to-day living that other people seem to enjoy.

Envy is first cousin to coveting and either state leaves a person
discontented. Whereas covetousness desires the possessions or
attainments of others in the hope of having them for itself, envy
does not wish so much to take for itself as it wishes to take away
from others. The desire of the "evil eye" is to see mishap and misfor-
tune visited upon those who are envied, to see the rich man lose his
wealth, the desired woman her beauty, the "normal," contented
family its happiness.

As sensitive beings, Fours are troubled by such emotions. This is
not surprising, for they are "feeling types," though feeling types with
a pronounced, subjective approach to other persons and themselves. Even so, they try hard to understand why they are the way
they are—why they envy, why they are depressed, why they are "different"—though tending all the while to emotional rather than
rational conclusions.

According to a perceptive observer, the melancholic personality
(to which the average to unhealthy Four is closely related):

1. Bullinger, *Number in Scripture,* 123.

47

is surely more self-centered than any of the other temperaments. He is inclined to that kind of self-contemplation which paralyzes his will and energy. He is always dissecting himself and his own mental conditions, taking off layer after layer as an onion is peeled, until there is nothing direct and artless left in his life; there is only his everlasting self-examination. This self-examination is not only unfortunate, it is harmful. Melancholics usually drift into morbid mental conditions. They are concerned not only about their spiritual state; they are also unduly concerned about their physical condition. Everything that touches a melancholic is of prime importance to him, hence no other type can so easily become a hypochondriac.[2]

By inhabiting a wing of the emotional or "heart" triad, Fours absorb the attitudes of others, though sometimes in a highly subjective manner. By internalizing perceived unacceptable and threatening attitudes, they are left anxious and out of balance, tempted to withdraw from others to shield their fragile emotions. Yet even as they withdraw, they grasp the facts of a social situation. Their immediacy of self-awareness (albeit overly subjective) is a pronounced trait, as well.

This aptitude for insight, this instinctive ability to bypass the discursive process, is a valuable gift. According to C. G. Jung, "The peculiar nature of introverted intuition . . . produces a peculiar type of man: the mystical dreamer and seer on the one hand, the artist and the crank on the other. The artist might be regarded as the normal representative of this type."[3] In the words of William Hazlitt, they have an "Intuitive perception of the hidden analogies of things."[4]

According to enneagram pioneer Claudio Naranjo, Fours can be subject to "sexual envy," an inclination to partake of aspects of the opposite gender. To Naranjo, this envy, experienced by both men and women, is "striking in the case of the counter-sexual identification underlying homosexuality and lesbianism." He says such pref-

2. Ole Hallesby, *Temperament and the Christian Life* (Augsburg Publishing House, Minneapolis, 1962), 43–44.

3. *Psychological Types,* 401.

4. Source unavailable.

erences are "more frequent in ennea-type IV than in any other character."[5]

As heart types dwelling next to the head center, Fours are also lovers of beauty, in both art and nature. Frequently refined and mannered, they are sensitive to stimuli both exterior and interior; "special," cultivated, they channel their inner turbulence into elegant expressions. There is indeed an artistic temperament at work. Even when not artistically gifted, they generally like to be surrounded by beautiful things and to decorate their dwellings tastefully.

Fours are inveterate "romantics." The prosaic ups and downs of everyday life do not provide them with the intensity they seek. They have little urge "to blossom where they are planted." Rather, they are fascinated by the exotic, the faraway, the fanciful, the adventurous, the hard-to-get. They withdraw from the world in its concrete and quotidian realities, withdraw from the mundane circles in which "lesser beings" live their lives. They are preoccupied with romantic love, too, and search after the ideal mate.

Not surprisingly, unhealthy Fours tend to be snobs. The snob has a self-conscious sense of superiority, built upon an inner doubt as to his or her real worth. Fours have such doubts in plenty. In compensation, they may exhibit an over-refinement, a showy sensitivity, aimed at distancing themselves from common mortals. Predictably, they maintain a keen interest in social and class relationships, an interest that points to the concerns of an envious nature. It is in their envious mode, from behind their façade, that Fours observe others keenly—then demean those others by belittling their humble concerns.

Artists by temperament, aware of the figurative and symbolic realms beneath the surface of things, Fours sometimes become artists in fact, translating their inner dramas into the productions of a poet or novelist, painter or sculptor. It is the self-revealing side of the Four that prompts the creative effort. Through this side of their

---

5. *Ennea-Type Structures, Self-Analysis for the Seeker* (Gateways/IDHHB, 1990), 69, 71.

nature, they marshal a talent for self-expression. Their churning emotions are given shape and scope. The original work that ensues is a vital expression of who they are, deeply connected to their sense of worth. Thus, the Four who is an artist comes to terms with himself by creating a work of art that expresses the inner being in an outward form.

To seek—as well as to create—the beautiful: to this the cultivated Four aspires. And to this there is more wisdom than less sensitive souls might think. In defense of the Four as dreamer, as seeker after apparent will-o-the-wisps, one might ponder the concept of *sehnsucht*, the German term for longing, nostalgia, deep yearning, "sweet melancholy." In his *English Literature in the Sixteenth Century*, C.S. Lewis says that *sehnsucht* "would logically appear as among the sanest and most fruitful experiences we have," for the object of longing "really exists and really draws us to itself."[6] Here, *sehnsucht* links us to the "Other," to the Divine Being in whom one's restless heart may find rest. In this, there is a sort of poetic proof of divine reality. "Lewis makes clear his belief that a desire for God does support the idea of his existence."[7]

Introverts as well as individualists, Fours are at home in their inner universe, marching to the beat of their own drum. They often see themselves as tragic, misunderstood figures, entitled to inhabit—and to enjoy—a sub-world of sadness and loss, to which they have been driven by the cold, cruel world. In this they are like the old Romantics of art and literature, proud beings too sensitive for this mortal coil, dwelling in twilight lands of impracticality and loss.

The average to unhealthy Four has in fact a deep discontent with his finiteness, with his limited nature. There is at work within him a deep rebellion, an unwillingness to admit his mere humanness before the Creator. There is a desire to be the center of his own self-centered self, a desire to be autonomous, a desire to be disconnected from the transcendent realm that limits him. Yet these are desires whose satisfaction is existentially impossible, inasmuch as God

6. Corbin Scott Carnell, *Bright Shadow of Reality: C.S. Lewis and the Feeling Intellect* (Eerdmans, Grand Rapids, Mich., 1974), 137.
7. Ibid., 140.

alone is the ultimate object of His human creatures. In rebelling thus, Fours refuse to love God enough to be contented, refuse to be thankful for the many gifts that he has given them.

Owing to these traits and the unhappiness they bring, Fours can become self-loathing, hence, at their worst, tempted to abuse themselves with drugs or unbridled sensuality. They may experience temporary, inverted pleasure from the pain and humiliation they inflict upon themselves, but their brooding thoughts and foolish actions plunge them ever deeper into misery. At their lowest level, they watch the great parade of the world as it marches by, leaving them alone and undeveloped, looking in from the outside. In their isolation, they refuse the healing that could be theirs by confiding in a trusted friend, by cultivating a deeper spiritual life. Inasmuch as they see themselves as defective, as not "measuring up," they feel their suffering is justified.

With life at low ebb, the tragic sense comes into full play. Their sense of loss takes on dramatic force; they become lost souls, acting the part in all respects. Moods fluctuate even more than usual. Increasingly helpless, they seek someone to cling to. They hold onto relationships that are frustrating, making an already bad situation worse. They may evoke the pity of others, and may indeed be cared for, but they end by resenting their caretakers.

Joseph, favorite son of the patriarch Jacob (Israel), bears the marks of a Four. He of the "richly ornamented robe" thought himself special and so did his father. Not surprisingly, this state of affairs antagonized his brothers.

Joseph the dreamer was among life's intuitive types. His dreams, dramatic in nature and clear in their message (they informed him he was superior to his brothers—and even to his father), were not only self-important but prophetic. Indeed, the time would come when his family would bow before him. In the meantime, his siblings hated this dreamy loner, who stayed at home while they grazed the flocks far away. When they got the chance, they stripped him, threw him in a cistern, and sold him to a passing caravan.

Thereafter, Joseph was taken to Egypt, where he was bought by Potiphar, captain of the guard. Despite his diligent and honorable service and the success it brought him, he found himself falsely accused of making advances towards the mistress of the house. Thus he was arrested—but not abandoned; the Lord was with him. He managed to thrive even in prison, where his dreams foretold the future yet again. Word of his gift reached Pharaoh, who asked him to interpret a dream. Joseph did so, explaining that it meant there would be seven years of plenty, followed by seven years of want. He advised Pharaoh on how best to prepare for these events. As a result, the Hebrew outsider was advanced to high office, where he served as Pharaoh's vizier. By his policies in the years of plenty, he assured that everyone would have enough to eat in the years of famine—and he made Pharaoh rich in the bargain.

Joseph suffered but never lost faith. He trusted God to redeem him and He did. He governed Egypt wisely and, eventually, was reconciled to his brothers. When they abased themselves before him, before this man of dignity and power, he was reduced to tears. In the end, he forgave them their sin against him. "You intended to harm me, but God intended it for good, to accomplish what is now being done, the saving of many lives" (Genesis 50:20). Here, Joseph spoke like an integrated Four, hence displaying the wisdom and objectivity of a One, able to discern the ways of the Lord who had been with him in his many travails, always working for good.

A measure of "alienation" is needed for moral renewal and spiritual progress. The heroes of Scripture, indeed, the true heroes of any age, are to one degree or another (Joseph included) alienated from the culture of their day, from the lure of expediency, hedonism and materialism. Perhaps more than any other type, Fours are aware of this alienation, and of the tensions that come in its wake.

As alluded to here, alienation is not referenced in the pathological but in the moral sense, as a partial and necessary estrangement from self, others, and one's surroundings. Such estrangement makes clear to the sensitive soul how "out of joint" the world is, of how rife with corruption, conformity and cruelty. Should one make peace with such a world? Should one make peace with the people who *do* make peace with such a world? Indeed, should one make peace with one's self, a self that is complicit in the world's deeds? A measure of healthy alienation is necessary, towards self and others, to prevent acquiescence to the herd mentality and the deeds that follow in its wake.[8] "Dear friends ... as aliens and strangers in the world, abstain from sinful desires, which war against your soul" (1 Peter 2:11).

Even so, Fours need to make common cause—albeit a discerning common cause—with others. They need, if they are believers, to take their place in the Body of Christ, in the *ecclesia,* among "the called out ones," and to learn that "the body is a unit, though it is made up of many parts; and though all its parts are many, they form one body" (1 Corinthians 12:12). They need to learn that "God has arranged the parts in the body, every one of them, just as he wanted them to be" (v. 18). God has made provision for his servants, he has set aside a place, prepared a path, set a task from all eternity. A part to be played awaits the Four, a part that will not smother creativity but one that will allow creativity to achieve its greatest scope. Hence, the Four is called to accept his concrete circumstances, to join with others, to apply his talent or talents. The Four is summoned to accept with gratitude his or her calling, rather than to pine continually for what never was and never will be.

Nonetheless, Fours find it difficult to draw close to others, especially when bad feelings have been aroused. Sensitive as they are, they tend to be easily hurt, and inclined to lick their wounds in private. Despite this tendency, they are best advised to engage others, to honestly express unhappiness toward them or to admit their own fault. Among the Eastern Fathers, an astute observer has this to say:

Association with others ... allows for a more rapid healing than does solitude, insofar as it constitutes for the individual a test in which he directly confronts the difficulties which are the source of his sadness, and so is more easily and rapidly cured. Otherwise he runs the risks that these difficulties might become more or less unconscious while continuing to remain active and thereby keep the person immersed in sadness. On the other hand, we know that the remembrance of injuries, resentment,

8. The matter is discussed at length in Walter Kaufmann's *From Decidophobia to Autonomy: Without Guilt and Justice* (Dell Publishing Co., Inc., New York, 1973), 140–147.

rancor and in general all that follows from anger, instead of spontaneously dissipating, have on the contrary a tendency to grow imperceptibly ... to spread like a venom and by degrees poison the entire soul.[9]

Thus the Four is well advised to associate more fully with others in the journey of life, to endure with others the difficulties and celebrate with others the joys that come his way. There is vanity in standing on the sidelines, observing others, tittering at their mishaps, demeaning their motives—and envying their triumphs. The Four needs to open up to the ordinary, to get his hands dirty in a good cause, to empty the ego *of* the ego, as it were, and to recognize that God—even God—has submitted himself to the confines of human life. God himself, in the person of Christ, took on the narrow, ordinary life that humans experience, took on the task of dying, a death far worse than others have to endure. Thus, the finiteness and mortality of the human condition have been shared by Deity himself.

Furthermore, the Four is advised to divert the uncontrolled emotions that spiral him into sin. He or she needs to harness them, to transmute them into good work and good works, and to avoid the pitfalls of sustained melancholy. The Four must not dream dreams only, but must *do.* It takes work to be happy, effort to be fulfilled—industry is the enemy of melancholy. In this, God cooperates; He has work for everyone to do, a place for everyone to be. "What makes life worth while is having a big enough objective, something which catches our imagination and lays hold of our allegiance; and this the Christian has."[10]

As in the Parable of the Talents, the single talent must be employed, not buried. To that end, the dreaming Four is wise to become more objective, more goal-oriented, more "earthy," though retaining the deep longings of the type. "The solid wisdom for man or boy who is haunted with the hovering of unseen wings, with the scent of unseen

9. Jean-Claude Larchet, *Mental Disorders and Spiritual Healing: Teachings from the Early Christian East* (translated by Rama P. Coomaraswamy and G. John Champoux, Sophia Perennis, Hillsdale, NY, 2005), 111.

10. J.I. Packer, *Knowing God* (InterVarsity Press, Downers Grove, Ill., 1973), 30.

roses, and the subtle enticement of 'melodies unheard, is *work*. If he follow any of those, they will vanish. But if he work, they will come unsought."[11]

Prone to melancholy as they are, Fours dread especially the final enemy, death, and brood on that enemy, aware the world is "ever passing." The Four is wise to face this enemy head on, to accept the inevitable, yet to do so in hope and faith: to trust in that which overcomes death. "Blessed are those who mourn, for they will be comforted" (Matthew 5:4). Fours must recollect in times of "fear and trembling" that "those who suffer he delivers in their suffering; he speaks to them in their affliction" (Job 36:15). Moreover, redemptive suffering fits a person for service, for "the Father of compassion . . . comforts us in all our troubles so that we can comfort those in any trouble with the comfort we ourselves have received" (1 Corinthians 1:3–4).

Fours realize their identity by "yoking" themselves to the Divine Principle; as Jesus said, "My yoke is easy, and my burden is light" (Matthew 11:30). In the East, a similar meaning attaches to the term *Yoga* ("union"), in which one enters the domain of Brahman, pervader of all things. According to Jesus, the yoke is offered "to all who labor and are heavy laden," for he will give them rest (v. 28).

In gaining control of their lives, Fours need not suppress their emotions; they do, however, need to channel them constructively, to combine achievement and art, labor and nostalgia, dream and reality. God is no stoic, nor should people be. Scripture says that God feels joy, sorrow, delight, love—even fear. The incarnate Second Person of the Divinity, Jesus of Nazareth, suffered the most acute anxiety in the garden, where he sweated drops of blood "Father, if you are willing, take this cup from me" (Luke 22:42).

The Four must be prepared, like Jesus, to drink of the cup, to offer willing service, in spite of anguish in the face of fear. The Four must learn to ask, with St. Paul, in faith: "Where, O death, is your victory? Where, O death, is your sting?" (1 Corinthians 15:55), and to echo with Paul the triumphant answer: "When the perishable has been clothed with the imperishable, and the mortal with immortality,

---

11. C.S. Lewis, *George MacDonald, An Anthology,* 109.

then the saying that is written will come true: 'Death has been swallowed up in victory'" (v. 54).

The Four who is spiritually justified needs to remember that he is "buried with Christ" in baptism, that he is in principle "dead to sin," that he will be raised with Christ; indeed, that he is raised daily in a foretaste of the heavenly things to come. There is a pattern of death and rebirth in all his days and to the end of his days.

A profound student of character, cited above, saw deeply into the melancholic temperament, empathizing and offering hope, underscoring a conviction that those who are more sensitive, inner-directed and imaginative may deserve the greatest honors. His words are relevant to the Four: "No one but a melancholic can appreciate fully the sufferings the melancholic must undergo. But remember, dear friends: The disciple whom the Lord loved was a melancholic man."[12]

Five: the Thinker

Avarice is the compulsion to . . . so completely surround and entrench and fortify oneself with material and psychological goods that one begins to unconsciously believe that one will never die, never be forced to let go of anything one has ever identified with. ∼ Charles Upton

THE FIVE, the "Thinker," is found in the Triad of the Mind. The number "is significant of Divine strength added to and made perfect in . . . weakness; of omnipotence combined with the impotence of earth; of Divine *favour* uninfluenced and invincible."[13] Dwelling in their heads and wary of the world, Fives indeed bear a measure of "weakness" and "impotence"—in spite of a strong, independent, and seemingly "omnipotent" mind—that only grace can overcome.

The capital sin of the type is greed or avarice. Their avarice is not for worldly goods but to know and understand things, to know and

12. Hallesby, *Temperament and the Christian Faith*, 59.
13. Bullinger, *Number in Scripture*, 135.

understand *everything*. Their avarice stems from fear of the world "out there" and the need to counter that fear. Thus, as C.G. Jung's *introverted thinking type*, they amass knowledge, develop complicated theories, and live a somewhat retired life. In doing so, they seek self-reliance and safety, while comprehending at arm's length the ever-threatening world.

Clear-headed and little given to wishful thinking, they are keen observers of what is happening around them. These traits, coupled with the ability to think abstractly, equip them to be scholars, intellectuals, researchers and analysts. They are always scanning people and places; they don't miss a thing. They evaluate and store the reams of data that pour in.

They are non-judgmental; they only want to know and to understand, to watch the passing scene, to "take it in"—even as they hide from it. What they observe they think about deeply and in detail. Yet the role of observer, played at the expense of a more rounded life, develops imbalance between thought and action. Even as their minds are active, emotions are bottled up and volition hindered. They are restrained in movement and posture as well.

Fives believe themselves misunderstood. After all, who can rise to their level of understanding? Who is worthy to share their thoughts? Unlike St. Paul, they do not feel "obligated both to the wise and the foolish" (Romans 1:14). The wise—or at least the intelligent—are enough for them. In their unhealthy states, they are isolated and anti-social.

The tendency towards isolation, which places them among the withdrawing types, is augmented by hypersensitivity. Even as they attempt to block out the intrusions of the world, the better to defend themselves against it, sensitivity to pain and noise remain marked traits. In addition, isolation fosters inner dangers, to "the Devil, who ever consorts with our solitude."[1]

Certain of the threats the Five perceives are, of course, all too real. The world is, in many respects, a dangerous place. By and large, however, it is projection—the ascription of their own thoughts and feelings to others—that is the source of fear. They read hidden

1. Sir Thomas Browne.

messages and dangers into the innocent remarks and actions of others, or into the random happenings of everyday life.

Unhealthy Thinkers, then, living in their minds and making little mark on the world, come to feel powerless, unable to act naturally and appropriately. Moreover, they become increasingly fearful as they withdraw from the challenges of life. Instead of honing skills for the real world, they become more and more preoccupied with their interior lives. Their spinning of theories and fantasies leaves them at a loss in dealing with outer realities. "The main picture that emerges . . . is that of a person who holds himself down to the extent of shriveling in stature, in order to avoid expansive moves."[2]

Anxiety, a diffuse feeling of dread, is the Thinker's particular form of fear and frequent companion. This feeling is fed by unconscious impulses and conflicts. He suffers from a simmering uneasiness, a lurking fear of catastrophe. Yet, as observed, he hopes by taking thought to keep this shadowy menace at bay. By acquiring and ordering and deploying an encyclopedic mass of knowledge, he hopes to inject an element of predictability into life, to outwit the ever-present dangers that threaten.

Greed, or avarice, the principle fault of the Five, is one of the seven "deadly" or "capital" sins. As indicated, Fives are not greedy for material goods. They are not greedy for power or prestige or great wealth, as Eights or Threes or other types might be. Instead, they are greedy for knowledge. Yet this leads to stinginess with time, money, emotions, possessions, discoveries and—even—thoughts. They want it all to themselves, the better to be safe from the dangers and intrusions of the world. As a result, they become minimalists, reducing needs and hoarding resources, becoming less dependent on others.

Owing to asocial tendencies, Fives display aloofness toward others. They are ill at ease with social niceties and humdrum activities, and quickly bored with small talk. Often socially awkward, they find attendance at public functions burdensome. They dislike the shallow chatter or "pointless" activities of a group. Like the introverted

2. Karen Horney, *Neurosis and Human Growth: The Struggle Toward Self-Realization*, 221.

thinking type they resemble, they can be "gauche in ... behavior, painfully anxious to escape notice, or else remarkably unconcerned and childishly naive."[3] While others engage in chit-chat, they keep their feelings to themselves and frequently lapse into total silence. ("This type tends to vanish behind a cloud of misunderstanding.")[4]

Not surprisingly, they avoid reaching out to others, let alone making a serious commitment to them. They prefer to spend time by themselves, in their "cave." There they analyze and assess the observations, facts and theories that fill their minds, an activity that escapes the hazards of personal contact even as it builds barricades of psychic defense. Predictably, they resent intrusions. Their cave is their castle.

Owing to their related absent-mindedness, they maintain only a secondary connection to everyday physical reality. They are not at home in their bodies. The world of the senses remains unexplored territory, all the better to avoid the dangers of the physical world. Their tendency to clumsiness and preference for thinking over doing follows naturally.

As individualists, outsiders and loners, Fives are detached from the customs and cant of society. They devise their own theories, form their own views. Owing to their detachment and social indifference, they often develop a wry sense of humor. Their breadth of knowledge, combined with keen observation, provides the data to pierce social pretense. Reserved though they are, they may burst into laughter at odd moments, catching others off guard and amusing the crowd—and themselves.

When they slip into unhealthy states, Fives become increasingly stubborn. They refuse helpful suggestions; they reject playing another's "game." Their minds take on a life of their own, becoming "overheated" as it were. Observes a seasoned student of the spirit:

His head is like a thought machine, operated by external force; it continues to think but is impotent to desist. ... [The] thoughts in his mind ... come to him in waves, rolling unceasingly day

3. C.G. Jung, *Psychological Types*, 385.
4. Ibid., 384.

and night. There is no way to terminate them. He is not aware that this is but the activity of the evil spirit. . . . [In] the case of these unmanageable thoughts it is not that his mind is grasping at something but rather that something is grasping his mind. In the natural course of events it is the mind which thinks about matters; now it is these matters which force the mind to think.[5]

In spiraling downward, Fives become cynical, distrusting selfless acts and disinterested points of view, and always suspecting a hidden agenda. They reject rules and conventions, become highly skeptical, and think themselves smart enough to see through everything. Thus they preserve their independence—and isolation. Neither God, nor man nor tradition has a claim on them. They "quench the Spirit" and life becomes increasingly empty.

Ultimately, the Thinker's strategy fails because his underlying problem goes deeper than he thinks. The problem is more than free-floating fear, attached first to this and then to that object. The problem is, at bottom, a sense of nothingness, a sense projected onto the world. He intuits the possibility of non-being, of the absence of all that is, be it good or bad, spiritual or material.

The Apostle Thomas fits the pattern of a Five. The name that tradition has given him, "Doubting Thomas," points to an element of skepticism in his nature. "Unless I see the nail marks in his hands and put my finger where the nails were, and put my hand into his side, I will not believe it." Thomas, who uttered these words, had been absent (how like a Five) when the resurrected Christ had first appeared to the rest of the disciples. When he was told the remarkable news, he expressed doubt. Even though present with Jesus when the master had performed miracles and wonders, he could not bring himself to believe in this, the greatest of miracles.

Why such doubt? Why, that is, beyond the intrinsic unlikelihood of such a stupendous event as the Resurrection? (But should it have been so unlikely in light of earlier events? The disciples had seen

5. Watchman Nee, *The Spiritual Man*, vol. 3 (Christian Fellowship Publishers, Inc., New York, 1977), 15.

Jesus raise the dead on more than one occasion). One could surmise the reason for Thomas's doubt was bitter disappointment, laced with inherent skepticism.[6] He had shared the joy and excitement of Palm Sunday, the triumphal entry into Jerusalem. Shortly thereafter, he had been appalled and dismayed by the events of the Passion. Consequently, everything appeared lost. He had hoped in vain. Thus, he chose to retreat to his own lonely center, to rely on his own resources. To do so he had to say "no" to reports of the Resurrection, to put the whole business out of mind, once and for all. The outer world—the world with all its pain and disappointment— would not be allowed to dash his hopes again. He had suffered enough.

Eight days later, Jesus returned to the disciples a second time. Thomas was summoned. Jesus offered tangible evidence to his skeptical follower: "Put your finger here; see my hands. reach out your hand and put it into my side. Stop doubting and believe." Thomas was overwhelmed, his defenses breached. In an instant, he was transformed. "My Lord and my God!" He had been offered proof of the Resurrection, the proof of the senses (and something more: the overwhelming authority and "presence" of Jesus). Tangible proof was possible to contemporaries of Jesus' days on earth, to such as Thomas. To the generations that have followed, belief has been mediated by Word and Spirit, through faith. "Because you have seen me," Jesus said to Thomas, "you have believed; blessed are those who have not seen and yet have believed." Blessed indeed are they who believe in these latter days, be they Fives or any other type.

The Varieties of Religious Experience presents the portrait of another Five, highlighting the skimping, minimizing (but in this case rather saintly) traits of the type. According to a memoir of the Unitarian clergyman and writer, William Ellery Channing, the young man seemed to have become incapable of any form of self-indulgence. He took the smallest room in the house for his study, though he might easily have commanded one more light, airy, and

---

6. As suggested in the chapter, "Hope When I Find It Hard to Believe," in J.I. Packer and Carolyn Nystrom, *Never Beyond Hope: How God Touches and Uses Imperfect People* (InterVarsity Press, Downers Grove, Ill., 2000).

in every way more suitable; and chose for his sleeping chamber an attic which he shared with a younger brother. The furniture of the latter might have answered for the cell of an anchorite, and consisted of a hard mattress on a cot-bedstead, plain wooden chairs and table, with matting on the floor. It was without fire, and so cold he was throughout life extremely sensitive; but he never complained or appeared in any way to be conscious of inconvenience. "I recollect," says his brother, "after one most severe night, that in the morning he sportingly thus alluded to his suffering: 'If my bed were my country, I should be somewhat like Bonaparte: I have no control except over the part which I occupy; the instant I move, frost takes possession.'" In sickness only would he change for the time his apartment and accept a few comforts. The dress too that he habitually adopted was of most inferior quality; and garments were constantly worn which the world would call mean.[7]

At healthy levels of personality, Thinkers—such as William Ellery Channing—are busy with useful projects and ideas, thereby contributing something to the world. Even when healthy, though, they are identifiable by characteristic traits. In the workplace, for example, they are at their best when left alone, as they resent close supervision. The boss, if he is wise, discovers "they are best put in a room alone and allowed to play"—the better to tap their creative juices. Once motivated, they doggedly pursue goals. They are innovators, problem-solvers; ready to break new ground, eager for challenges.

At their best, they are bold thinkers, devising complex theories to interpret and order disparate facts and phenomena in surprising ways. They can turn an avalanche of data into a coherent and meaningful body of knowledge. They synthesize unlikely ideas, observing connections that others have missed. They seek patterns and meanings beyond the obvious. They may develop a predictive ability, "prophetic" in a natural sense, discerning the outcome of events. Such insight can lead to increased understanding of others, hence a much-needed link to the rest of humanity.

Thinkers need to make a leap of faith, to transcend the discursive mind, to open the windows of the soul to the breezes of Spirit. For

7. William James, 300–301.

"of making many books there is no end, and much study wearies the body" (Ecclesiastes 12:12). They need—in faith—to ask, seek and knock, in hope of being answered, and found, and the door opened. For "without faith it is impossible to please God, because anyone who comes to him must believe that he exists and that he rewards those who earnestly seek him" (Hebrews 11:6). By faith, they must enter the circle in which, as St. Paul says, "we live and move and have our being."

For no man is an island: no man is cut off from the Source of being. For all their gifts of intelligence and airs of autonomy, Fives cannot, by themselves, fathom their essential being or the universe in which they dwell. A woodsman cannot cut off the limb on which he sits and expect to remain connected to the tree; no more can a Five sever his being from the root of all being and expect to be nourished by it. A direct, living relationship is needed. "Experimental knowledge of the truth as revealed to the heart of the individual directly by the Father is the only possible key to the kingdom of God."[8]

Ever-increasing knowledge on the horizontal plane—by itself—will never satisfy the Five, nor will it provide protection from social realities and natural calamities. Neither will the Five's own thoughts, no matter how clever and complex, lessen the anxieties within. Even knowledge of the Divine, apart from "heart" knowledge, will prove unhelpful in the end. For "light that is bound in the head to coldness must descend into the heart, to marry there the love, which is full of warmth and which languishes in the shadows."[9]

To attain balance, then, Fives must integrate head and heart, but by no means at the expense of the former. For if they become spiritual, they are frequently drawn to metaphysical knowledge; "simple faith" alone does not satisfy them. They are knowers primarily and believers secondarily. This is their gift. The ability to understand things metaphysically is a talent that must not be minimized, even

---

8. E. Y. Mullens, *The Axioms of Religion* (Judson Press, Philadelphia, 1908), 95.

9. Antoine Faivre, *Access to Western Esotericism*, quoting from Franz von Baader's *On the Biblical Concept of Spirit and Water* (State University of New York Press, Albany, 1994), 125.

as they come to realize that faith and knowledge are not, in themselves, opposed.

That being said, the normal order remains St. Anselm's *credo ut intelligam*—"I believe so that I may understand." Or, in the words of Karl Barth, "Faith, not reason, is the basis of Christian knowledge." Yet knowledge is vital—and Fives are abundantly equipped to assimilate it, in all its metaphysical rigor and beauty. In the mind of the Five, belief flowers into understanding, and life, enriched by spirit, becomes at last worth living.

Six: the Guardian

The fear of God makes one secure.
∼ Alī ibn Abū Tālib

ONE COULD SAY that Sixes are "all too human." After all, it "is the number of imperfection; the human number; the number of MAN as destitute of God, without God, without Christ . . . *man* was created on the *sixth day,* and thus he has the number *six* impressed upon him. . . . *Six,* therefore, is the number of *labour* . . . of man's labour as apart and distinct from God's rest."[1]

Though everyone is fearful at times, some types are beset by a higher level of fear than others (the Five, for example). Guardians, however, are not only fearful but keenly aware of being fearful. Located in the center of the Triad of the Mind, they are plagued by anxiety, a free-floating fear that overshadows daily experience. They are vividly aware of all the things that can go wrong, hence, they develop defensive strategies, ranging from subservience to authorities to habitual self-deprecation. They even engage in "magical thinking," believing their worst fears will fail to materialize if they "experience" them in a hundred imaginings instead.

Detached from "God's rest," Sixes are not only fearful of real and imagined threats but doubtful of their abilities and afraid of being

1. Bullinger, *Number in Scripture,* 150.

alone and disliked. Feeling "destitute of God," they find their ulti-mate authority on the human plane. They are ready and willing to do what human authorities expect of them, a strategy that ensures (they think) safety. Thus, Guardians avoid violating rules and cus-toms and identify with those who represent recognized standards. Yet, aware of their own secret temptations to deviate from the cus-tomary, they project those temptations onto others—and then judge those others harshly.

Though dutiful by nature, Sixes distrust other people. And why shouldn't they? They distrust themselves. Again, it's a matter of pro-jection, of seeing themselves in others. For that reason, they prefer impersonal and inflexible rules to the less predictable dynamics of personal relationships. Hence, security trumps the desire for easy relations with others.

In striving to do good things and to do them right, Sixes are beset by performance anxieties. When seeking the approval of others, they live in fear of mistakes, large and small. They repeat the same or sim-ilar questions again and again ("Is it okay? Shall we move ahead, then?"), to ensure acceptance of their suggestions and decisions.

Yet Guardians can be "clubby" and engaging, loyal to the church, the party, the company, with a marked talent for hospitality. Their "naïve, spontaneous, genial nature opens doors and hearts."[2] They are quick to criticize or minimize themselves, not only to make oth-ers feel at ease but to short-circuit criticism. "Sorry, I just threw this together at the last minute. I hope you like it." Dare one disagree?

To remain in their comfort zone, Guardians view issues in black and white. Hence, inconvenient facts that disturb their cherished beliefs are dismissed. Likewise, owing to a suspicion of change, they cultivate a temperamental conservatism. When questions arise as to a course of action, they ask how things were done in the past. This avoids breaking new ground, reduces the need for choice, and allays anxiety. Moreover, they are adept at interpreting every jot and tittle of the rules and thereby able to forestall, at least temporarily, the anxiety caused by uncertainty or ambiguity.

2. Ole Hallesby, writing of the "sanguine" type, elements of which are found in enneagram type Six, in *Temperament and the Christian Faith*, 16.

Sixes find it hard to initiate projects. They are hesitant, tentative, lacking in confidence. Even a course of action that appears eminently do-able stirs fear; fear that the status quo may be altered. "Better the devil you know...." They are paralyzed by inner resistance; they develop a talent for postponing their lives.

Despite their fears, Guardians are unafraid to act within well-defined limits. Tentative when out of their element, they can become strong and stubborn within a prescribed setting, especially if in a position of authority. Unyielding and defensive, they may threaten others in the name of the in-group. They can become bullies, sparing others as little as they have spared themselves. Moreover, in seeking to allay their fears, they may act in ways opposite to normal inclinations. Hence, when "counter phobic," they take surprising risks, such as challenging their superiors, or engaging in a dangerous sport, all in the hope of putting nagging anxieties out of mind.

The Six is related to C.G. Jung's *Introverted Feeling Type.* According to Jung, the type consists principally of women, a view not shared by enneagram theory. His words on the subject, however, are to the point, especially as he describes the suspicious and combative nature of less than healthy specimens of the type. Thus, he says, they may suspect others "are thinking all sorts of mean things, scheming evil, contriving plots, secret intrigues, etc. In order to forestall them, [they are] obliged to start counter-intrigues, to suspect others and sound them out, and weave counterplots.... Endless clandestine rivalries spring up, and in these embittered struggles [they] will shrink from no baseness or meanness, and will even prostitute [their] virtues in order to play the trump card."[3]

Sensitive to their faults—faults often enough undetectable by others—Sixes find it hard to accept at face value the praises they receive. Owing to self-opposition, their self-esteem is at the mercy of both other persons and their own accusatory conscience. Feeling pressured, they strive all the harder to do the "right thing," to obey the rules, to follow the correct course. In doing so, they further stimulate their anxieties, further kindle their inner doubts.

3. *Psychological Types,* 391.

Perhaps surprisingly, Sixes have a philosophical turn of mind, with a talent for seeing the pros and cons of an issue. "Should I, or shouldn't I?" Their self-doubts and endless inner questioning hone the skills of logic: like a competent lawyer, they argue both sides of the case before the inner judge. Hence, on one side they search for absolutes and display the passion of the "true believer," on the other, they remain ambivalent—or even rebellious.

Their ambivalence, clearly the defining characteristic of the type, splits the ego between fear and counter-fear. As such, they are replete with contradictions, swinging pendulum-like from one pole to the other. They support authority and are submissive to it—yet frequently fear and resent it. They obey—yet secretly wish to rebel. Traditional to the core, they weary of tradition. They long for security but take foolish risks. Their anxieties, then, impel them first one way, then the other: at one moment toward dependence, the next toward defiance.

An insightful expression of the "divided self" (in the phrase of William James) can be found in the words of Annie Besant, the English Theosophist:

I have ever been the queerest mixture of weakness and strength, and have paid heavily for the weakness. As a child I used to suffer tortures of shyness, and if my shoe-lace was untied would feel shamefacedly that every eye was fixed on the unlucky string; as a girl I would shrink away from strangers and think myself unwanted and unliked, so that I was full of eager gratitude to any one who noticed me kindly; as the young mistress of a house I was afraid of my servants, and would let careless work pass rather than bear the pain of reproving the ill-doer; when I have been lecturing and debating with no lack of spirit on the platform, I have preferred to go without what I wanted at the hotel rather than to ring and make the waiter fetch it. Combative on the platform in defense of any cause I cared for, I shrink from quarrel or disapproval in the house, and am a coward at heart in private while a good fighter in public. How often have I passed unhappy quarters of an hour screwing up my courage to find fault with some subordinate whom my duty compelled me to reprove, and how often

have I jeered at myself for a fraud as the doughty platform com-
batant, when shrinking from blaming some lad or lass for doing
their work badly. An unkind look or word has availed to make me
shrink into myself as a snail into its shell, while, on the platform,
opposition makes me speak my best.[4]

In summary, the Six is a conflicted individual, loyal but sometimes defiant, timorous but sometimes aggressive, rule bound but
sometimes rebellious. Yet if he is healthy, the Six can be an impres-
sive figure. He excels at being affectionate, dependable, loyal, willing
to soldier on for the good of the cause and of the people with whom
he is aligned. When he is healthy, he learns to trust himself and others and to affirm, instead of negate, his gifts. He can learn to laugh at
his fears and make decisions for himself, instead of always relying on
the authority of others.

In the Apostle Peter, we find a predictably inconsistent Six, phobic and counter phobic by turns. On the one hand, he was a man of
courage and conviction, quick to act, aggressive, and a gifted leader.
At the time of Jesus' arrest in the garden, he drew his sword and cut
off the ear of a member of the arresting party. Though ordered by
Jesus to sheathe his sword, he had shown a willingness to fight for
his master. Earlier, he had made it known (embarrassingly, it turned
out) that he was willing to die rather than disown Jesus. In the Acts
of the Apostles, he preached a Spirit-empowered sermon on the day
of Pentecost. Later, he defied the Jewish high council, expressing
keenness to obey God rather than men, regardless of cost.

Peter: loyalist, team player, guardian, and, on one occasion, a
judgmental enforcer of the rules. Devoted to his master, he tried—
wrong-headedly—to dissuade Jesus from his path of suffering.
Throughout the Gospels, he gravitated towards leadership but did
not claim the prerogatives of power. Again, in the Acts of the Apostles, he displayed a fierce indignation in judging Ananias and Sap-
phira, for their deception regarding the sale of property.

4. William James, *The Varieties of Religious Experience*, 168–169. Quotation is
from Annie Besant's *Autobiography*.

On the other hand, Peter's phobic side was clearly evident. After proclaiming his loyalty unto death, he disowned Jesus three times, an act of cowardice predicted by his master. Peter showed weakness of character in a later incident, too, when he reversed his position on a contested issue owing to fear of the Judaizers (to those, that is, who believed that circumcision was necessary for salvation).

The Bible puts fear in perspective. In well known words, in Proverbs 1:7, it lays the foundation for a Scriptural view of the subject: "The fear of the LORD is the beginning of knowledge, but fools despise wisdom and discipline." This speaks to the fear that overcomes fear. Yet "fear of the LORD" does not imply a cringing timidity but rather a reverence and submission to the One who loves and guides his people. By displacing more and more of their fears on Him, Sixes lessen their anxieties.

The prophet Isaiah affirms God's caring and supportive intentions: "You will keep in perfect peace him whose mind is steadfast, because he trusts in you" (26:3). Or this: "Do not fear, for I am with you. . . . I will strengthen you and help you; I will uphold you with my righteous right hand" (41:10). God can be trusted to ease the afflictions of an anxious mind. With His "right hand," the hand of power and deliverance, He is utterly reliable. The mind that finds rest by trusting in Him becomes "steadfast," hence less agitated by the oscillations of fear and self-doubt.

Jesus encourages the fearful to ease their fears by setting proper priorities and focusing on the present. In the Sermon on the Mount, He addresses those who belabor the countless "what-ifs" of life. "But seek first his kingdom and his righteousness, and all these things [food, drink, clothing and the other necessities] will be given to you as well. Therefore do not worry about tomorrow; for tomorrow will worry about itself. Each day has enough trouble of its own" (Matthew 6:33–34).

Sixes need to cultivate a life of prayer, to raise in prayer "the empty hands of faith." A life of prayer, of sincere and personal communication with God, can ease the anxieties that oppress them. The Apostle Paul put it this way: "Do not be anxious about anything, but in everything, by prayer and petition, with thanksgiving [how important "thanksgiving" is], present your requests to God. And the peace of God, which transcends all understanding, will guard your hearts and your minds in Christ Jesus" (Philippians 4:6–7). Prayer, an intimate relationship with God, and petition, the boldness to make requests of God, are presented as keys to spiritual and psychological balance.

As intimated, "thanksgiving" is a third key. One who counts his or her blessings, trite as this may sound, will discover much to be grateful for. The peace thereby attained "transcends," goes "above and beyond," thus surpassing human understanding. "For you did not receive a spirit that makes you a slave again to fear" (Romans 8:15). It is not a "psychological peace" only, a peace centered in the human faculties. It is a spiritual peace, as well, a peace that can be known when a believer is assured his sins are forgiven and that he can cast his cares on the Lord.

Yet prayer is not a magical formula. It does not always "work." One does not always receive what one asks for. Yet "unanswered" prayer can be a means of sanctifying a believer, of building patience and courage. Anxiety may continue its unsettling ways, yet even here there is a silver lining. "Some people feel guilty about their anxieties and regard them as a defect of faith. I don't agree at all. They are afflictions, not sins. Like all afflictions they are, if we can so take them, our share in the Passion of Christ."[5]

In Christian tradition, the obedience and dutifulness exemplified by Sixes are virtues. "Everyone must submit himself to the governing authorities, for there is no authority except that which God has established" (Romans 13:1). However, as we have seen, these virtues can be put to unworthy uses. It is one thing to be an obedient and useful citizen in civil society, another to be enslaved by the petty rules and rituals of pharisaical religion. The Six must be alert to the danger. Personal integrity must not be sacrificed willy-nilly to dubious authority, in matters of civil life or in matters of faith. In both, it is the principle that is to be followed, not a narrow and literal rendering of it. "A religion which commands awakens revolt, if there are only commands. Christianity as a personal religion begins with

5. C. S. Lewis, *Letters to Malcolm, Chiefly on Prayer* (Harcourt Brace Jovanovich, New York and London, 1964), 41.

faith. Its method of growth is fellowship with God, entering into his plans, grasping his aims."[6]

Jesus reverses the values of the generality of men. Thus, he teaches his followers humility, not pride. "You are not to be called 'Rabbi,'" he says, "for you have only one Master and you are all brothers. And do not call anyone on earth 'father,' for you have one Father, and he is in heaven. Nor are you to be called 'teacher,' for you have one Teacher, the Christ. The greatest among you will be your servant. For whoever exalts himself will be humbled and whoever humbles himself will be exalted" (Matthew 23:8–12). The greatest of Christ's followers are called to be "servants," just the role for a healthy Six. In turn, good servants make good leaders.

Moreover, owing to a change of heart and mind, the fetters of misinterpreted and rigidified law are loosened. Sixes find "their attempts at obedience are now joyful, integrated in a way that was never true before. Sin rules them no longer. In this respect, too, they have been liberated from bondage."[7] Thus they are freer, lighter, more joyful. Obedience—hitherto a heavy burden—becomes at last a welcome restraint, an easy yoke.

Above all, they develop independence of mind and a healthy self-reliance, even while—paradoxically—relying more fully on God. "But the first and finest expression of Christ's lordship over the individual believer is in the gift of autonomy to him. Christ discovers each man to himself and starts him on an autonomous career, but never for a moment does he relax his grasp upon that man's conscience or life. Yet nothing thrills men into such a sense of freedom and power."[8] Christ appoints "kings and priests unto God," releasing them from the bondage of a fearful self, freeing and empowering them for a fuller life, to the benefit not only of others but to themselves as well.

---

6. E. Y. Mullens, *The Axioms of Religion*, 28–29.

7. J. I. Packer, *Concise Theology: A Guide to Historic Christian Beliefs* (Tyndale House Publishers, Inc., Wheaton, Ill., 1993), 173–174.

8. Mullens, 128.

Seven: the Adventurer

Every desire is insatiable, and therefore is always in want.
~ Sextus the Pythagorean

SEVEN IS FROM the root *savah*, *"to be full or satisfied, have enough of*. Hence the meaning of the word 'seven' is dominated by this root, for on the *seventh* day God rested from the work of Creation."[1] These comments penetrate to the heart of the Seven, or "Adventurer," as he or she is called here. For the type combines a never-ending quest to "be full or satisfied" with a never-ending inability to find the satisfaction that is sought.

Sevens are tempted chiefly by gluttony, yet another of the capital sins. Owing to it, they inordinately chase after pleasure, experience and adventure. They are the ultimate consumers, ever in search of the finest foods, the most fashionable apparel, the latest hobbies, the current "in" places. Sensuous and sensual, they are the "pagans" whom Jesus cites in Matthew 6:31–32, who spend their time on what they shall eat and drink and wear. For pagans "run after all these things." So do Sevens, to disguise and suppress their anxieties. In doing so, they channel their urges, conflicts and fantasies into frequently undisciplined and undigested action.

Located in the Triad of the Mind, next to the "doing" or "gut" triad, they recall the sanguine disposition of Galen's ancient typology. In speaking of it, C.S. Lewis said the "Sanguine man is plump, cheerful and hopeful. A fifteenth-century manuscript symbolizes [the type] by a man and a woman, richly dressed, playing on stringed instruments on a flowery place."[2] Optimistic "head types" that they are, they indeed seek pleasure and avoid pain. Yet in doing so, they often "leap before they look," neglecting to count the cost. Focused in the moment, savoring the here and now, or contemplating future pleasures (which is a pleasure in itself), they remain in

1. Bullinger, *Number in Scripture*, 167–168.
2. *The Discarded Image: An Introduction to Medieval and Renaissance Literature* (Cambridge University Press, UK, 1998), 171.

perpetual motion mentally and physically. Above all, they fear empty moments, as they threaten to remind them of the less appealing aspects of life. Hyperactivity is their panacea. As Pascal put it:

Nothing is so insufferable to man [and most of all, to the Seven] as to be completely at rest, without passions, without business, without diversion, without study. He then feels his nothingness, his forlornness, his insufficiency, his dependence, his weakness, his emptiness. There will immediately arise from the depth of his heart weariness, gloom, sadness, fretfulness, vexation, despair.[3]

To counter such emptiness, Sevens seek with gusto the things they want, even as they hold at arm's length the serious questions they hesitate to ask. Clearly, they are averse to self-examination. They prefer to keep busy, thereby protecting themselves from empty moments that beckon them to brood on life's unpleasant realities. Their favorite book title might be Willem van Wulfen's *The Sybarite: A Guide to the Ruthless Enjoyment of Life.*

As observed, Sevens are avid consumers, in thrall to the latest fashions in behavior, clothing, food and travel. In pursuit of the world's goods, they turn from the sober realities that might temper their indulgences. In this, they resemble Kant's "light-blooded" type who "is carefree and full of expectation; he attributes great importance to everything for the moment, and at the next moment he may not give it another thought.... He is a good companion, jocular, and high-spirited; he does not like to attribute great importance to anything... has everybody for a friend.... Business tires him, and yet he is restlessly busy with things that are mere play, because this provides change."[4]

"Good companions" that they are, Sevens eagerly share their pleasures with others, inviting them to join the circle of delight. Every day is a rolling party, demanding companions. To live is to play. Not surprisingly, their aptitude for selling the good life extends beyond the personal, to commercial, political and show business

3. Blaise Pascal, *Pascal's Pensees* (E. P. Dutton & Co., Inc., New York, 1958), 38.
4. Immanuel Kant, *Anthropology from a Pragmatic Point of View*, 198.

pursuits. Ever the smiling salesmen, they are skilled at the selling of images, services, products . . . and themselves.

Sevens are notable as "quick studies," able to acquire skills rapidly by immersing themselves in the moment. They have no fear of the new, as long as it promises an exciting challenge or a pleasurable romp. Their grasp of the material world, and their ability to use it skillfully, is singular. This sure and steady handling of material reality recalls the *Extraverted Sensation Type* of C.G. Jung: "No other human type can equal [this] type in realism. His sense for objective facts is extraordinarily developed."[5] Although able to assimilate skills rapidly, he is tempted to become an undisciplined dilettante, displaying a permissiveness toward himself (and others) that causes him to shy from discipline. Despite his remarkable array of talents, he despises restraints and refuses the hard work required to turn an aptitude into a developed skill.

Predictably, Sevens are talented storytellers, witty and detailed in their renditions. They combine this gift with their wealth of experience, thus enhancing entertainment value. Here as elsewhere, they steer clear of the unpleasant facts of life, preferring instead bits of humor and action drawn from the surface of things. This fills the void, as does their penchant to hum, sing, tap the table, play music, or otherwise create miscellaneous noise to counter the threat of emptiness.

Not surprisingly, the Adventurer can develop a rebellious side in opposition to the legitimate constraints of the social environment. Here again, the attempt to remain free of burdensome duties, as well as the avoidance of unpleasant realities, reflects a less-than-serious attitude toward life. It is the attitude of one contemptuous of "square" or "straight" behavior. It is the attitude of one who shirks his duty; of one who "gets away with things."

In his unhealthy states, the Seven increasingly refuses to face suffering, deprivation or sacrifice. In compensation, his activities become increasingly manic, but his pleasures, ever more elusive. He runs faster and faster, like a hamster on a wheel. He fills his growing inner vacancy with drink, drugs, food or any other means available.

5. *Psychological Types,* 363.

In time, he suffers the more or less delayed effects of chronic indulgence, which takes a toll on health and appearance, two of the type's most important concerns. The remedy involves some form of self-limitation, but self-limitation is anathema to a Seven.

To be fair, such shallow and sensuous activities represent only one side of the Seven, and only some Sevens at that. One can find in the type a disciplined and purposeful individual, as well, even as the charm and high spirits remain. Healthy Sevens are refreshing and enthusiastic, friendly, helpful, likely to attract others to share the good times and the good things of life. They learn to appreciate rather than merely consume the gifts and talents they have. Outgoing and uninhibited, they remain "the life of the party."

David, "the sweet singer of Israel," was a flawed figure who embraced his share of adventure—and folly. A Seven among Sevens, he was—despite his flaws—a man "after God's own heart." Though a man of humble beginnings, he "rose to the top;" a shepherd boy, he ruled his people. Handsome, passionate and skilled, he expressed his vibrant personality as poet, musician, warrior and sovereign. Filled with a lust for life, he danced before the Ark of the Covenant, he composed Psalms, he was zealous in war. He was a well-rounded man of spontaneity, depth and courage.

Once accustomed to the throne and its prerogatives, however, David's character weakened. When from his balcony he saw the beautiful Bathsheba, wife of Uriah the Hittite, he determined to have her, even as Uriah and the king's army were away at war, risking their lives for the king. Yet adultery was only the beginning of David's treachery, of the shameful course of events in which he arranged for the death of Uriah in battle. In sum, "David took Bathsheba (thus, by theft, breaking the eighth commandment) and got her pregnant (thus breaking the seventh) and then to avoid scandal arranged for her husband Uriah to be killed (thus breaking the sixth), and it all began with David coveting his neighbor's wife, in breach of the tenth [commandment]."[6]

---

6. J. I. Packer, *I Want to be a Christian* (Tyndale House Publishers, Inc., Wheaton, Ill., 1977), 304. Only when exposed by the prophet Nathan did the king acknowledge his sins in this sordid episode.

In the years that followed, David met with success and failure, joy and sorrow. Yet through it all, he remained in his heart of hearts "right" with God, no matter how counterintuitive that might seem. His faith was strong, his repentance sincere, his devotion enduring. Though his sins were scarlet and his excesses many, he was promised an eternal dynasty. From his line would be traced the Messiah: from his legacy, the idea of a great king restored.

To be transformed—or transmuted—into healthier persons, Sevens need to rein in their compulsive behaviors, to "put on the brakes." Their relentless activity must be curbed; besetting sins, identified and addressed. They are advised to "Renounce the sin that holds you fast—and then you will recover your faith! If you dismiss the word of God's command, you will not receive his word of faith. How can you hope to enter into communion with him when at some point in your life you're running away from him?"[7]

A more reflective temper must be cultivated. "When you are on your beds, search your hearts and be silent" (Psalm 4:4). Folly and overindulgence must be seen for what they are: attempts to evade God, finitude and death. Such temptations must be resisted. Proverbial wisdom sketches the penultimate state of those who fail to do so: "How I hated discipline! How my heart spurned correction! I would not obey my teachers or listen to my instructors. I have come to the brink of utter ruin" (Proverbs 5:12–14).

Attempting to rein in the passions demands a disciplined exercise of the will. This is true especially for Sevens, given their embrace of all things pleasurable. For them, the attainment of freedom from overindulgence is a difficult feat; a lifetime's habits will not change in a day. For "the yoke of the passions is much heavier and more difficult to throw off than that of the most cruel tyrants."[8] Yet they need not destroy the passions, only "watch over them and repress excess in them, because all excess is vicious."[9]

---

7. Dietrich Bonhoeffer, *The Cost of Discipleship*, 73.

8. Fabre d'Olivet, *The Golden Verses of Pythagoras*, translated by Nayan Louise Redfield (BiblioBazaar, Charleston, SC, 2008), 157.

9. Ibid. Here the word "vicious" refers to vice in general rather than to that which is savage or ferocious.

In learning to discipline themselves, Sevens must learn that the world is something other than a round of novelties and pleasures. For it is, all too often, a school of patience and a vale of tears. And yet, "Do not make light of the Lord's discipline, and do not lose heart when he rebukes you, because the Lord disciplines those he loves, and he punishes everyone he accepts as a son. Endure hardship as discipline; God is treating you as sons. For what son is not disciplined by his father?" (Hebrews 12:5–7).

Life itself—especially the less pleasant side of it—teaches Sevens the lessons they need to learn. For

> Sufferings test and awaken generous sentiments; [while] pleasures promote and fortify base instincts. Sufferings arm against pleasure; enjoyment begets weakness in suffering. Pleasure squanders; pain ingarners. Pleasure is man's rock of peril; the pain of motherhood is woman's triumph. Pleasure fertilizes and conceives, but pain brings forth. Woe to him who cannot and will not suffer; he shall be overwhelmed by pain. Nature drives unmercifully those who will not walk; we are cast into life as into an open sea: we must swim or drown.[10]

On their face, such words are repellent to a Seven, yet they represent the pattern of sanctification. For God himself is not only tender and merciful, he is just and severe. He subjects His wayward creatures to the circumstances that mold them into the saved creatures He wishes them to become. The process hurts; it is a slaying of the ego. The Bible does not minimize the hurt. "No discipline seems pleasant at the time, but painful. Later on, however, it produces a harvest of righteousness and peace for those who have been trained by it" (Hebrews 12:11). St. Paul asserts much the same principle, observing that we "rejoice in our sufferings, because we know that suffering produces perseverance; perseverance, character; and character, hope" (Romans 5:3–4). Furthermore, he adds, our "present sufferings are not worth comparing with the glory that will be revealed in us" (8:18).

10. Eliphas Lévi, *The History of Magic* (Samuel Weiser, Inc., York Beach, Maine, 1999), 50.

More than any other type, the Seven must learn that grasping for happiness and pleasure is the surest way to miss them. In fact, one of the first conditions of happiness is the renunciation of the superficial and perpetual need to feel happy at all times. But this renunciation "cannot spring from the void; it must have a meaning, and this meaning cannot but come from above, from what constitutes our reason for being."[11]

To the Seven (and to the Three, as observed earlier), conversion may bring a period of euphoria, a short-lived state of elation to confirm the baby believer in faith. The joy of "new birth," with special signs and providences, may highlight the time of transition. In the period that follows, however, challenges and difficulties can be expected. After all, the believer is called to witness, to worship, to serve . . . to sacrifice. His walk will include seasons of joy, yes, but labor and strife as well. The Seven, and not the Seven alone, needs to face the sterner side of discipleship. Sacrifice, then, "the taking up of the cross," will be part of the journey. Yet it brings compensations with it. "I do not know how it comes about, but it is nevertheless certain that man gains in stature by voluntary suffering and that general opinion itself thinks the more of him for it. . . . Has any libertine ever discovered a rich courtesan, who sleeps on feathers at midnight, happier than the austere Carmelite, who rises and prays for us at the same hour?"[12]

Like all of the other types, Sevens run the race that is marked out for them. As they face the sometimes unhappy realities of life—face them in faith as they run the providential course—they find themselves increasingly liberated from their former compulsions. They learn to take the long view, to live by the Spirit, to no longer slavishly gratify "the desires of the sinful nature" (Galatians 5:16). For when "one does a shameful thing with pleasure, the pleasure passes and the shame remains. When one does an excellent thing with great trouble and labour the pain passes and the excellence alone remains."[13]

---

11. Frithjof Schuon, *Survey of Metaphysics and Esoterism,* translated by Gustavo Polit (World Wisdom Books, Bloomington, Indiana, 1986), 218.

12. Joseph de Maistre, *The Works of Joseph de Maistre,* translated by Jack Lively (Macmillan, New York, 1965), 261.

13. Fabre d'Olivet, 201–202.

Henceforth, they find themselves building on rock, not sand. In the past, they have consumed ephemera that promised lasting pleasure. Redeemed, they look elsewhere to find fulfillment. "Taste and see that the LORD is good; blessed is the man who takes refuge in him" (Psalm 34:8).

Eight: the Leader

He who conquers others is strong;
He who conquers himself is mighty.
~ The Tao Te Ching

"IN HEBREW the number eight is ... (Sh'moneh), from the root ... (Shah'meyn), 'to make fat' ... 'to super-abound.' As a participle it means 'one who abounds in strength,' etc. As a noun it is 'superabundant fertility' ... as a numeral it is the super-abundant number."[1]

There is nothing particularly fat about Type Eight, inasmuch as "fat" indicates obese or overweight in today's usage, rather than the "richest or choicest part," "firm" or "plenteous," as it does in the Bible reference above. There *is* in the Eight, however, a "super-abundance" in abundance. The Eight is solid, strong, tough-minded, commanding and confrontational, fully equipped to face and master his or her circumstances.

On the wing of the Triad of the Will, Eights are seekers of intensity. Lust is their capital sin: the quest for power, wealth, sex and control, their touchstones. In pursuit of goals, they are brave, tenacious and enterprising. C. S. Lewis notes that "choleric" types, who much resemble Eights, "dream of thunder and of bright, dangerous things, like arrows and fire."[2] For his part, Immanuel Kant says the choleric "is hot-tempered and ... is quickly ablaze like a straw fire. ... His activity is impetuous, but not lasting. ... He likes to be

1. Bullinger, *Number in Scripture*, 196.
2. C. S. Lewis, *The Discarded Image*, 172.

the chief who makes the decisions, but does not like to carry them out. Consequently, his dominant passion is ambition."[3]

The intelligence of Eights is practical, applied, instinctive. Their minds do not spin in circles; they do not second guess themselves. Predictably, they are not detail-oriented, nor given to puzzling over particulars. They will sketch out a plan on a napkin over lunch, thereafter leaving the fine-tuning to others. Their contribution is vision, energy and drive. In all of this, they know what they want and they work hard to get it. They embody an "expansive solution: the appeal of mastery."[4]

It follows, then, that Eights are always prepared to act, to "follow a hunch." Aware the first instinct is often the right one, they "cut to the chase," disregarding irrelevant details and side issues and forging ahead. They make a decision "and keep their eye on the ball," while others become distracted and lose their way. Like the *Extraverted Intuitive Type*, they submit their decisions "to no rational judgment and [rely] entirely on [their] nose for the possibilities that chance throws in [their] way."[5]

As noted above, Eights strive to attain wealth, power and control, the resources they need to reach their chief goal: self-reliance. To attain self-reliance, they can be cunning and sarcastic, pushy and domineering. They neither trust others nor submit to them. The more successful they are in achieving self-reliance—and often they are very successful indeed—the more arrogant and overbearing they may become.

In keeping with the foregoing, Eights enjoy competition in its many forms, be it the physical demands of a contact sport or the matching of wits in social or business settings. They like to put pressure on others, to focus on their vulnerabilities, "to see what they are made of." There is a sheer joy in action, in living intensely, in winning. By contrast, inactive Eights are unhappy Eights. Without projects, they "chafe at the bit," becoming restless and irritable.

3. *Anthropology from a Pragmatic Point of View,* 199–200.
4. Karen Horney.
5. C.G. Jung, *Psychological Types,* 368.

"Because he is always seeking out new possibilities, stable conditions suffocate him."[6]

In the modern era, there is great stress on physical and practical toughness, material achievement and mastery of the environment, at the expense of interior development. It is a world in which Eights—and not Eights only—thrive. "In the past most societies tried systematically to discourage somatotonia [W.H. Sheldon's typological formulation most resembling the Eight]. This was a measure of self-defense; they did not want to be physically destroyed by the power-loving aggressiveness of their most active minority, and they did not want to be spiritually blinded by an excess of extraversion."[7] Just so. The modern age *is* characterized by "excess of extraversion."

Eights can be heroes. Samson, the strong man of the book of Judges, is an example. A heroic but flawed figure, a Hercules among the Hebrews, his career traces the path of an archaic Eight, with the strengths and weaknesses of that formidable type.

Samson was consecrated a Nazirite ("No razor may be used on his head . . . [he is] set apart to God from birth."—Judges 13:5), chosen to deliver Israel from the Philistine enemy. He lived his life independently, courageously, violently, yet as a protector of the weak and the downtrodden. He was coarse and lustful, visiting a prostitute (chapter 16) and demanding a Philistine woman for his wife ("Get her for me. She's the right one for me."—14:3). He displayed cunning and verbal wit. He was a contriver of riddles.

Samson's superhuman strength accounted for fabulous deeds against the Philistines, whom he slew in their thousands. He killed a young lion as well with his bare hands and burned the fields and vineyards of his enemies by out-foxing the foxes. But the great warrior met his match in the crafty Delilah. Her plotting led to the shearing of Samson's hair, followed by his capture and blinding. Bound in shackles, he was set to grinding in the prison. Yet the hair of the Nazirite grew again. While his enemies mocked him in their temple, God "remembered" him and gave him back his strength. In

6. Jung on the *Extraverted Intuitive Type,* ibid., 370.
7. Aldous Huxley, *The Perennial Philosophy,* 161.

his final act, he pulled down the temple upon his foes, killing "many more when he died than while he lived" (16:30).

Such was Samson: warrior, hero, chosen vessel. Yet a man, too, of cunning, lust and vengeance, coarse and impetuous. Samson was light and dark, courage and folly. In spite of his vices, he was redeemed. A frightening figure, yes, but a figure some distance above the depths to which the type can sink.

At their lowest levels, Eights become ruthless, merciless and destructive. They may develop a sense of omnipotence and delusions of grandeur. There is a growing obsession with extravagant achievements. They trample on anyone in their way. In spiraling out of control, they become vengeful and sadistic, ready to intimidate, humiliate or physically injure anyone with the temerity to oppose them.

At the other end of the spectrum, the Eight becomes magnanimous. A born crusader, he seeks justice and protects the weak. He still aspires after mastery, but for the good of others and not for himself alone.

His ability to lead is evident in the bold, steadfast and courageous manner in which he faces challenges, in which he inspires others to follow his example. What he lacks in talent he makes up for in grit. "When the going gets tough, the tough get going." Abounding in stamina, he never gives up and seldom slows down.

Healthy Eights demonstrate their strength through a surprisingly tender side of their nature. This may be connected to the forgotten "child" who lives within. Perhaps by discovering this veiled and vulnerable self, they are able to reach out to weak and helpless others who need their succor and protection. Thus the erstwhile tyrant becomes—from time to time at least—the embodiment of benevolence.

Even in expressing this kinder, gentler side of themselves, Eights find it difficult to show emotion. Warm and welcoming they are not. Yet they expect others to interpret their actions as based in love. Others do not always do so, and the Eight may feel unappreciated.

At their healthiest, Eights become big-hearted, merciful, ready to take the weak and downtrodden under their wing. In this, to their

credit, they seek justice ("For the LORD is righteous, he loves justice; upright men will see his face." Psalm 11:7). Moreover, they learn
to forgive the occasional injury and insult, no longer harboring
petty resentments. They are, after all, strong and resolute; they can
"take it."

Eights like to prove their mettle in the physical realm, to "build
big" in tangible ways, to demonstrate strength for all to see. As
means to independence and security, as pathways to inflating their
egos, such activities may indeed bear fruit. Yet in regard to spiritual
life, they clearly "miss the mark" (the very definition of *hamartia*,
sin). Scoring points in the "world"—attaining high political office,
becoming a tycoon, commanding a military campaign, or exercising
some lesser role of leadership—is not, in and of itself, either good or
bad for the soul's health. Rather, the soul's health depends on one's
relationship to the spiritual order, on the disposition of one's essentially secret and interior unfolding.

Where one's heart is, one's treasure is. When Eights put "heart
and soul" into worldly enterprises, when they are consumed by
them without remainder, they have departed from the Way, the
Truth and the Life, settling instead for that which moth and rust do
corrupt. The Eight receives no enduring peace from worldly
achievement. "What does a man get for all the toil and anxious striving with which he labors under the sun? . . . Even at night his mind
does not rest" (Ecclesiastes 2:22–23). Though pleased briefly with
his latest achievement, he restlessly turns to new schemes and con-
quests the moment opportunity allows.

Eights need to recognize that wealth and power are properly
means, not ends. For human essence, the *imago Dei* or image of
God, partakes of immortality. It transcends the works of the flesh,
the achievements of the passing world. It is, therefore, vital to enter
into that which lasts. Paradoxically, this may bring an increase in
earthly blessings (as observed of the Three): "Honor the LORD with
your wealth, with the first fruits of all your crops; then your barns
will be filled to overflowing, and your vats will brim over with new
wine" (Proverbs 3:9–10).

The spiritual man or woman of strong personality is called to
protect the weak and to seek justice, to be a tribune of the down-

trodden. At the same time, he or she is to cultivate a life of self-control, channeling forceful instincts into good works and away from temptations to aggression. "Refrain from anger and turn from wrath; do not fret—it leads only to evil. For evil men will be cut off, but those who hope in the LORD will inherit the land" (Psalm 37:8–9). The spiritual relationship—leading to peace—is to be given priority at all points. Inclinations to anger and vengeance, conversely, are to be mortified; that is, "put to death," no matter how justified they might seem to be. Believers are advised to "Make every effort to live in peace with all men and to be holy; without holiness no one will see the Lord" (Hebrews 12:14).

When their tempers flare, Eights are well advised to take a breath and "count to ten," as the conventional adage puts it. For they need perspective on themselves and the situations they find themselves in. They need to know that a non-aggressive response to a provocation can have an impact greater than an aggressive one. A peaceful word to an adversary, under the right circumstances, may very well "heap burning coals on his head" (Romans 12:20); that is, impart a burning sense of shame. A mild reply can work a sort of "spiritual jujitsu," throwing an opponent by the weight of his own intent. Such is God's preferred method: to short-circuit violence by breaking its patterns of escalating conflict. "A patient man has great understanding, but a quick-tempered man displays folly" (Proverbs 14:29).

In the teaching of Christ, the command to treat others in loving ways ("So in everything, do to others what you would have them do to you, for this sums up the law and the prophets."—Matthew 7:12) goes to the greatest of lengths: "But I tell you: Love your enemies and pray for those who persecute you, that you may be sons of your Father in heaven. He causes his sun to rise on the evil and the good. . . . Be perfect, therefore, as your heavenly Father is perfect" (5:44–45). The "enemy," then, should be treated with mercy—be he evil or good, righteous or unrighteous—just as the Father would treat him. The world teaches "an eye for an eye;" the Eight exacts an eye for an eye, even an arm or a leg for an eye. This inverts the Christian rule. Eights should be "perfect" in treatment of their enemies. (Here, "perfect" means not without fault but rather, as the Greek literally says, "brought to completion.") It is out of such com-

84

pletion, or state of fulfillment and wholeness, that Eights find the peace to extend peace to others, even enemies.[8]

One finds similarly irenic teaching in St. Paul, where the Apostle urges the following: "Don't have anything to do with foolish and stupid arguments, because you know they produce quarrels. And the Lord's servant must not quarrel; instead, he must be kind to everyone. Those who oppose him he must gently instruct in the hope that God will grant them repentance leading them to a knowledge of the truth" (2 Timothy 2:23–25). "Gently instruct" are the key words. By nature, Eights are not inclined to be gentle.

To urge the love of one's enemies clearly does not imply one does not *have* enemies, only that they should be treated according to the law of love. The Eight, because of his strength and natural combativeness, is tempted to return violence for violence, as he is likely to prevail. But the teaching of Jesus and Paul, advising non-retaliation, is actually designed to benefit the Eight (and other types, both dominant and compliant), because no one wins spiritually in avenging an insult. Those who initiate and those who respond to violence both incur "cosmic debts," as teachers as diverse as Confucius and the authors of the Bible make plain. For sin reverberates to the "third and fourth generations," and can be broken only by refusal to acquiesce in its temptations. "Forgive us our debts," Jesus prays. Inasmuch as energy can be neither created or destroyed, the fruits of non-retaliatory action on the earthly plane translate into rewards on the eternal plane. The reward is delayed but it is real; it is only "bumped up a level," as one stores away "treasures in heaven" by abstaining from sins on earth.

In recommending a prayer to cholerics, Alexander Whyte expressed (in fine Victorian flourish) the desiderata of an integrating Eight:

> Lord, let me be ever courteous and easy to be intreated. Never let me fall into a peevish or contentious spirit. Let me follow peace with all men, offering forgiveness, inviting them by courtesies, ready to confess my own errors, apt to make amends,

---

8. These teachings, we believe, legislate not for governments but for individuals.

and desirous to be reconciled. Give me the spirit of a Christian, charitable, humble, merciful and meek, useful and liberal, angry at nothing but my own sins, and grieving for the sins of others, that, while my passion obeys my reason, and my reason is religious, and my religion is pure and undefiled, managed with humility, and adorned with charity, I may escape thy anger, which I have deserved, and may dwell in thy love, and be thy son and servant forever.[1]

Integrating Eights realize that God provides the only firm foundation for living. Next to this, the material foundation of self-reliance crumbles, the power-ego is humbled. "Humble yourselves, therefore, under his mighty hand, and he will raise you up in due time" (1 Peter 5:6). God will "raise up." God will use the Eight's strength at the time of His choosing. The Eight at rest in this knowledge feels the peace that passes all understanding.

Nine: the Peacemaker

I have so much to do that I am going to bed.
~ Savoyard proverb

NINE "is the *last* of the digits, and thus marks the *end;* and is significant of the *conclusion* of a matter . . . it is thus significant of the *end of man,* and the summation of all man's works. . . . It marks the completeness, the end and issue of all things as to man—the judgment of man and all his works."[2]

Type Nine *is* a conclusion and a summation of all things human; indeed, the prototype of the types, according to at least one enneagram authority. Richard Rohr, in his *Discovering the Enneagram: An Ancient Tool for a New Spiritual Journey,* co-authored with Andreas Ebert, says, "It's no accident that the NINES are situated at the vertex

1. *The Treasury of Alexander Whyte,* 249.
2. E.W. Bullinger, *Number in Scripture,* 235.

of the Enneagram, because in a certain way NINE describes the original and unspoiled human essence. We would probably all be NINES, if we hadn't grown up in a technologically 'civilized' world."[3] That being said, the Nine is a prototype under judgment, as are all things regarding "man and . . . his works." For like other types, the Nine is wounded in his nature; one finds no "unspoiled essence" this side of the Fall.

Located in the center of the Triad of the Will, Nine is a "gut" type between Eight and One. It relates to C. G. Jung's *Introverted Sensation Type;* it exemplifies one of Karen Horney's "self-effacing solutions." Strong-willed like its adjacent types, it expresses the capital sin of sloth. Phlegmatic and often withdrawn, it is willful in maintaining stasis, like a motorist braking and accelerating at the same time. In the unflattering words of Thomas Elyot, the phlegmatic—of which the Nine is an example—is characterized by "colour white . . . sleepe superfluous . . . dremes of things watery or of fish . . . slowness . . . dullnesses of lerning . . . smallness of courage."[4]

Immanuel Kant assesses the type more happily, which he says is

not stirred easily or quickly, but, if slowly, then persistently. He who has a good dose of phlegm in him warms up slowly; but he holds the warmth longer. He does not get angry easily. . . . His fortunate temperament takes the place of wisdom, and even in ordinary life people often call him the philosopher. By virtue of this temperament he is superior to others without offending their vanity. Frequently he is cunning, because all the bullets and missiles fired at him bounce off him as from a sack of wool.[5]

Nines long to attain union, balance and harmony with people, nature, God and the cosmos. This longing reflects a deep current in human nature. In seeking to attain it, however, Nines can become passive, resigned, neglectful, undeveloped and obstinate. Hence, they often are life's late starters, characterized by lack of motivation

---

3. The Crossroad Publishing Company, New York, 1992, 162.
4. C. S. Lewis, *The Discarded Image,* 173.
5. *Anthropology from a Pragmatic Point of View,* 200–201.

and a minimum of goals. "Such a type can easily make one question why one should exist at all."[6] In contemplating action, they believe "others can do it better." When they do take the field, they are unclear about goals and strategies. In their least healthy states, they are conflicted, divided, immobilized, in spite of their longing for unity.

Sloth, which today indicates mental or physical laziness, and puts one in mind of the slow-moving arboreal creature of the same name, was called *accidie* in the Middle Ages. At that time it had a more comprehensive and deeper meaning. It involved a refusal of God's grace, of His offer of help, opportunity and growth. "Accidie is partial consent to non-being, striking a bargain with insignificance."[7]

Fathers of the Eastern Church recognized the traits of this spiritual ailment in great detail. In discussing it, they observed its correspondence "to certain states of sloth and to a state of ennui," as well as its link to "disgust, aversion, lassitude ... dejection, discouragement, apathy, torpor, nonchalance, drowsiness, somnolence, and heaviness of both body and soul." Accidie, they taught, "can even induce a person to sleep when he is not really tired."[8] Clearly, it is a condition more complex than sloth in the narrow sense. For its part, the Nine incorporates both traditional and current meanings. In the words of Alexander Whyte, addressing the phlegmatic humor,

> Sloth sums up, in one short and expressive word, the bad side of this temperament. Some part of what we call sloth in men is, no doubt, in fairness to be set down to such a phlegmatic constitution that it would take the will and the energy of a giant to overcome it. There are men of such a slow-working heart, their blood creeps through their veins at such a snail's pace, their joints are so loosely knit, and their whole body is so lethargic, that both God and man must take all into consideration before they con-

6. C.G. Jung, on the *Introverted Sensation Type* in *Psychological Types*, 395.
7. William S. Stafford, *Disordered Loves: Healing the Seven Deadly Sins* (Cowley Publications, Boston, Mass., 1994), 113.
8. Jean-Claude Larchet, *Mental Disorders and Spiritual Healing: Teachings from the Early Christian East*, 102.

demn them. And when we say sloth in this case, we still take into account all that can be said in extenuation, and the phlegmatic man will not be blamed for what he could not help. He will be blamed and chastised only for what he could well have helped if only he had resolved to help it. At the same time, sloth is sloth, laziness is laziness, whatever your temperament may be. Laziness, indeed, is not of the body at all; it is of the mind."[9]

To assure inner peace, the Nine maintains modest and regular habits. There is a clinging to "security blankets," a special enjoyment of games, hobbies, and forms of passive entertainment, such as operating a computer or viewing television. Nines often collect knickknacks or enjoy tinkering with gadgets. They appreciate homely surroundings, where they dwell amidst the familiar and the comfortable. They are happy to identify with a group—a family, club, sports team—to obtain a sense of self. Safe in their routines and protected environments, they find themselves "oriented amid the flux of events not by rational judgment but simply by what happens."[10]

Average Nines tend to be socially stable, owing partly to their unreflective and undeveloped inner life. They avoid the effort of hard, critical thought, accepting instead the commonplaces of their milieu. They are undisturbed by self-examination. Yet "men are without excuse" (Romans 1:20); the "once-born" must face up to spiritual obligations; inner work is required. They need to ask, seek and knock, to investigate spiritual dimensions within and without. But like the *Introverted Sensation Type*, the average Nine "is uncommonly inaccessible to objective understanding, and . . . usually fares no better in understanding himself."[11]

In the effort to remain undisturbed, Nines can be stubborn and "passive-resistant" (or petulant and "passive-aggressive") when it comes to fulfilling their obligations, whether or not the demands are

9. *The Treasury of Alexander Whyte*, 252.
10. C. G. Jung, on the *Introverted Sensation Type* in *Psychological Types*, 395.
11. Ibid., 397.

reasonable. Yet, if nothing else, they are difficult to exploit. They balk at making decisions and meeting deadlines; they resist if they believe they are being asked to do too much. When they do consent, they perform what is asked and no more. It is not for them to go above and beyond the call of duty.

In spiritual matters, Nines are content "to wait on the Lord." They heed not the Word, with its droll example of diligence: "Go to the ant, you sluggard. Consider its ways and be wise!.... How long will you lie there, you sluggard? When will you get up from your sleep?" (Proverbs 6:6–9). Unlike the ant, average Nines are little moved by inner resolve. They rely instead on external forces to nudge them into action.

Despite their sluggish tendencies, Nines expend plenty of energy, paradoxical as it may seem. In doing so, they exercise their will, albeit in a largely instinctive and unconscious manner. Most of the energy is devoted to remaining immobile. As noted above, they push on the brake and the accelerator simultaneously. Or, to change the metaphor, they "run fast" only to remain in place: expending all their energy on routine tasks while neglecting more useful allocations of time, leaving themselves subject to fatigue and depression.

Owing to the equilibrium of sloth, they may speak in a monotone and show little expression or animation in the face. They often listen and respond to others inattentively. They may say "yes" but do not really mean it. Instead, the "yes" is a tactic to avoid conflict. This can lead to misunderstandings and strained relationships. "The type becomes a menace to his environment because his total innocuousness is not altogether above suspicion."[12]

Unhealthy Nines refuse to recognize painful facts. By this means, they escape intimations of failure and evidence of underdevelopment. They escape as well, for a time, the anxieties such thoughts are bound to provoke. They remain out of touch with the springs of action that motivate others and could be used to motivate themselves, inhabiting instead their personal Walden Pond of peace and simplicity.

12. Ibid.

Disintegrating Nines can become angry and defiant, reacting against those who try to coax them into a more directed and energetic mode of living. Yet try as they might to avoid acknowledging their increasingly unhappy situation, they may reach the moment of truth in which they can no longer repress their failures and self-defeating strategies. The earlier, easygoing self may become anxious, agitated, overly emotional, possibly turning to drink or drugs for escape.

Of course, Nines have their virtues, too, with generosity and liberality among them. They are able, also, to endure trying situations with patience and courage, to sustain others in trouble, and to serve as support for those close to them. They are good-natured, calm and reassuring. They are steady under pressure. Also, owing to their dispassionate temper, they make excellent mediators. Moreover, as they integrate to a healthier self, they become more assertive; they become "doers of the word, not hearers only."

At their healthiest, Nines become a "presence in the room," ready to play a constructive role in society. At the same time, in the inner life, they attain peace, unity and equilibrium, their most longed-after qualities. No mundane substitute, no matter how legitimate in itself, can take their place, for they alone provide to the Nine "the peace that transcends all understanding."

The patriarch Abraham bears the marks of the Nine. Raised amidst the idolatry of Ur of the Chaldees, "Abram" showed himself passive and obedient before the revelatory God of the Bible. In response to a theophany, he left his native land and sought a promised destiny. A city-dweller, he became a nomad, drifting with his flocks and herds, assured by the Divine Word of countless descendents and a homeland for his people.

This phlegmatic progenitor of the Hebrews demonstrated time and again his inclination to pursue peace and harmony, whether for good or ill. When conflict developed between his herdsmen and the herdsmen of his nephew, Lot, Abraham allowed his nephew to choose the better part of the land. "Let's not have any quarreling between you and me" (Genesis 13:8). So, too, when the Lord made clear his determination to destroy Sodom, Abraham pleaded on behalf of the city's righteous inhabitants, evincing his pacific, merciful tendencies. When, on two occasions, he feared for his life at the hands of foreigners, he showed his passivity—indeed, his fear and timidity—by attempting to pass off his wife Sarai (Sarah), as his sister, an act of expediency if not cowardice. On the other hand, in keeping with his stolid nature, he could show a cool head and stubborn determination. He demonstrated courage and tactical skill when he led his armed men in the attack that defeated the four kings in the Valley of Siddim.

Abraham showed himself to be as pliable in the hands of Sarah as in the hands of God. At the instigation of his wife, he had intercourse with Sarah's maid, Hagar, to assure an heir. When she became pregnant, Hagar "began to despise her mistress" (Genesis 16:4). Irate, Sarah blamed Abraham for the unhappy situation. In typically meek fashion, he bore his wife's anger and gave Sarah permission to do what she wished. As a result, the maid was banished for a time. (Of her illegitimate union with Abraham, Ishmael was born.)

In due course, God fulfilled his promise to Abraham and Sarah by giving them a son of their own, Isaac. At the time Isaac was weaned, Sarah observed Ishmael mocking her son. She ordered Abraham (with "backup" from God) to expel Ishmael and Hagar from their midst. Abraham—conflicted, passive but ever obedient—did so.

Not surprisingly, Isaac was the apple of Abraham's eye. Yet when God demanded the sacrifice of Isaac—in one of the Bible's most harrowing passages—Abraham showed himself characteristically pliant, though undoubtedly anguished. He expressed his faith, his trust, in God to the greatest extent. In the end, divine intervention prevented the sacrifice of the boy, even as Abraham was utterly vindicated in God's sight. "Now I know that you fear God" (Gen. 22:12).

The healthy Nine is one thing, the unhealthy, another. Even the Nine who is spiritually committed is not free from danger. Sloth and passivity can trap the unwary. For

It is possible for a consecrated Christian to be deceived into passivity for some years without ever awakening to his dangerous plight. The degree of inactivity will increase in scope until he suffers unspeakable pain in mind, emotion, body and environment. To present the true meaning of consecration to these ones thus becomes vitally important. The knowledge of truth is absolutely necessary for deliverance from passivity, without which freedom is *impossible*. We know that a believer falls into passivity through deception but this latter in turn is caused by a lack of knowledge. The very first step to freedom is to know the truth of all things: truth concerning cooperation with God, the operation of evil spirits, consecration, and supernatural manifestations.[13]

To know "the truth of all things"—the truth of all things relevant to the spiritual malady at issue—is indeed a vital first step. Such truths are embedded in the precepts of Scripture. For the "law of the Lord is perfect, reviving the soul. The statutes of the Lord are trustworthy, making wise the simple" (Psalm 19:7). Such benefits are mentioned elsewhere, as well: "I have more understanding than the elders, for I obey your precepts" (119:99). And then there is this: "Though I am lowly and despised, I do not forget your precepts" (Psalm 119:141). Even the most self-deprecating of Nines can take heart from such words. Obedience to God, and the integrity, focus and strength that issue from it, stirs the phlegmatic soul to action. "Never be lacking in zeal, but keep your spiritual fervor, serving the Lord" (Romans 12:11).

According to the Apostle Paul, writing in 1 Corinthians, everyone in the community of believers is a vital member of the Body of Christ. The key to service is availability. Nines need to be "present" in spirit, soul and body, to take their rightful place, to let their light shine and their good deeds be manifest. For "Whoever sows sparingly will also reap sparingly, and whoever sows generously will also reap generously" (2 Corinthians 9:6). Nines need to persist, to be hopeful, to be watchful, to be in the thick of things. For "Unlike orchids [Christians] do not grow as hothouse plants. Jesus did not live the life of a hothouse plant, evading life's abrasiveness, and he does not intend that his disciples should either."[14] Nines need to

13. Watchman Nee, *The Spiritual Man*, vol. 3, 120.
14. J.I. Packer, *Rediscovering Holiness* (Servant Publications, Ann Arbor, Mich., 1992), 188.

unearth their buried talents and put them to use in ways that serve others and develop themselves.

In meditating on the Lord's Prayer, C. S. Lewis discovered a surprise meaning in the petition, "Thy will be done." By emphasizing the last two words, he realized that much that needed to be done was to be done by God's servants, himself included. "The petition, then, is not merely that I may patiently suffer God's will but also that I may vigorously do it. I must be an agent as well as a patient. I am asking [in prayer] that I may be enabled to do it."[15]

In becoming such an agent, the Nine is called to confront with steadfast courage the difficulties, challenges and troubles of life, both exterior and interior. This is never easy, especially for a type inclined to accidie. For in the words of a wise old divine, there is nothing

> we naturally dislike so much as "trouble". . . . We secretly wish we could . . . be good by proxy, and have everything done for us. Anything that requires exertion and labour is entirely against the grain of our hearts. But the soul can have "no gains without pains."[16]

In tandem with others, the Nine is called to action, to step into his or her role on the stage of life and to become something other than a passive observer. The world is not to be considered a zero-sum game, nor a necessitarian straightjacket; it abounds with possibilities, openings, opportunities. By transmuting spiritually, Nines link to the creative and causal energy in both the Center, and in their center. They begin to walk in the paths prepared "before the foundation of the world," paths ever new, ever old, and ever open to the liberated soul.

15. *Letters to Malcolm: Chiefly on Prayer*, 25–26.
16. J.C. Ryle, *Holiness*, 69.

One: the Striver

To fall into the sin of anger is to claim the divine right to determine what has the right to exist and what does not.

~ Charles Upton

"THERE CAN BE no doubt as to the significance of the primary number. It is the symbol of unity. . . . 'One' excludes all difference, for there is no second with which it can either harmonize or conflict."[1] Ones do indeed exclude "all difference," esteeming themselves keepers of the ONE RIGHT WAY. They do not "harmonize" with ease but "conflict" most certainly with others and themselves.

Fundamentally, they are strivers after truth and virtue, in brief, after moral perfection. Despite their all-too-human faults and failures, this deep-seated motivation animates them from first to last. For as "the flame of a torch tends always upward whichever way one turns it . . . the man whose heart is afire with virtue, whatever accident befalls him, directs himself always toward the end that wisdom indicates."[2] To vary the image, the One's principal motivation provides him with an interior gyroscope, drawing him back to the correct course every time he goes astray.

Melancholic and choleric by turns, Ones are found in the Triad of the Will. Owing to their root sin of anger, they are critical by nature. They are, when less than healthy, similar to C. G. Jung's *Extraverted Thinking Type*, a figure who combines the principled rationalist and the carping critic, who is a "sultry and resentful character. . . . Magnanimous as he may be in sacrificing himself to his intellectual goal, his feelings are petty, mistrustful, crotchety, and conservative."[3]

Even as Ones are afraid of being condemned, they are quick to condemn others. They project a sense of vileness onto their neighbors, and berate themselves with equal fervor. ("I do not know what

1. Bullinger, *Number in Scripture*, 50.
2. Fabre d'Olivet, *The Golden Verses of Pythagoras*, 202.
3. *Psychological Types*, 350.

95

the heart of a rascal may be; I know what is in the heart of an honest man; it is horrible."—Joseph de Maistre). Their stance is dualistic: their self-loathing is the inverse of their self-righteousness.

"In your anger do not sin" (Ephesians 4:26). Good counsel, yet Ones find it difficult to suppress resentment. At war with themselves, they are at war with others and anger "will out," if not in a tantrum then in facial tics, compulsive gestures, rigidity. They "stew in their own juices."

For his part, Immanuel Kant says the "heavy-blooded" melancholy, in which aspects of the One can be seen, "directs his attention first of all to difficulties, while the sanguine person relies on the hope of success. Therefore the melancholy person thinks deeply, just as the sanguine thinks only superficially. . . . [The melancholy is] uneasy, mistrusting, and critical, thereby also incapacitating him for joyfulness."[4]

Ones are impatient with both themselves and others. Instead of accepting the need for process in matters spiritual and practical, of step-by-step advance, they strive hurriedly for completion. Yet, as in spiritual alchemy, no substance can be made perfect without a long suffering. "Great is the error of those who imagine that the philosophers' stone"—that legendary preparation capable of transmuting base metals into gold or silver, and base souls into elevated ones— "can be hardened without first having been dissolved."[5] Beginnings, by their nature partial and imperfect, conflict with the One's psychic ideal. Hence Ones, discouraged by disorderly conditions, by the "dissolved substance" that is the necessary material of the step-by-step process of deliverance, find it hard to begin the "work," hard to get the flow of activity going. They aspire to get it right, *right now,* today, not tomorrow.

In fact, in making mundane if not spiritual decisions, the One usually *does* get things right, to the annoyance of others less particular. In the One's view, "lesser mortals" should follow his example, for

4. *Anthropology from a Pragmatic Point of View,* 199.
5. *The Spiritual Ascent: A Compendium of the World's Wisdom,* presented by Whitall N. Perry, quoting the hermeticist Henry Madathanas (Fons Vitae, Louisville, Kentucky, 2007), 125.

there are standards to be upheld; everyone should adhere to them, everyone "should get it right." Yet not everyone does get it right, not to the One's satisfaction. Thus Ones monopolize tasks and responsibilities, marginalizing others and tending towards "workaholism." ("If you want something done right, do it yourself.")

But this is shortsighted and unrealistic, unsatisfactory to themselves and others. Among other things, it heightens their awareness of how much they have to do and of how little time they have to do it in, thus adding unnecessary pressure to their lives. If they would integrate to a healthier self, they should seek out the help of others and work with them to develop their talents. As has been said, "Instead of doing the work of ten men, get ten men to work." A similar policy is suggested in the Bible, when Jethro, the priest of Midian, advised Moses to select judges to ease the burden of governing. Wisely, Moses accepted the advice of his father-in-law, to his and the people's gain.

Among other traits, the One's critical inner voice curbs spontaneity and causes him to interrupt himself, to correct his own speech and to argue against himself. This criticality reinforces the tendency to be judgmental and reductive, and relates Ones to the *Extraverted Thinking Type* who "elevates objective reality, or an objectively oriented intellectual formula, into the ruling principle not only for himself but for his whole environment. By this formula good and evil are measured, and beauty and ugliness determined. Everything that agrees with this formula is right, everything that contradicts it is wrong, and anything that passes by it indifferently is merely incidental." [6] Nonetheless, criticality has its advantages. Like the double-edged sword of the Word, Ones penetrate "even to dividing soul and spirit, joints and marrow" (Hebrews 4:12), drawing the sharpest distinctions, discerning right and wrong, just and unjust. They are lucid thinkers and rigorous reasoners (deductive in method), compelled to be honest. They see through the pretenses of the phony, they ferret out the deceiver.

In a related vein, they incline to scrupulosity, they "strain out gnats and swallow camels." They are sticklers for detail. Everything

6. *Psychological Types*, 347.

should be in its place, and there should be a place for everything. They apply their scrupulosity to mundane matters as well as to higher levels of concern, to spiritual practice and philosophical investigation. These latter disciplines, to please a One, must be consistent and accurate in all their parts; in short, they must be perfect.

Martin Luther, who suffered greatly from scruples, says in his *Commentary on Galatians* that his superior, Staupitz, was inclined to say, "I have vowed unto God above a thousand times that I would become a better man: but I never performed that which I vowed. Hereafter I will make no such vow: for I have now learned by experience that I am not able to perform it. Unless, therefore, God be favorable."[7] A good but flawed man, Staupitz expressed the wisdom of maturity, fully aware that grace alone would see him through.

Indeed, as with the other types, the One's sins, failures and mistakes have their place in the unfolding of personal destiny. It may seem like cold comfort at the time to a One with a tender conscience, but, in the end, even one's transgressions—if honestly repented of—are among the building blocks of the sanctified life. There is no evil that we do commit, rhymed Robert Herrick,

> But hath th' extraction of some good from it:
> As when we sin: God, the great *Chymist,* thence
> Drawes out th' *Elixar* of true penitence.[8]

Ones are incensed if things are not fair. They are seekers of justice, not only for themselves but for others, or in the name of an abstract ideal. They are steadfast for truth, even at their own expense. Extroverted thinkers, they are on a mission to reform, to "teach and preach," to witness to the truth as they see it. They wish things to be as they *should* be.

In the end, Ones are loathe to let go of their striving because they believe they must be perfect to be loved and accepted. The love of God for his wayward creatures; His reaching out to imperfect beings while they are yet sinners, are data of faith that elude them. Yet, in the divine economy, the faithful are saved by grace, through faith,

7. William James, *The Varieties of Religious Experience,* 129.
8. *The Spiritual Ascent,* 62.

and this not of themselves, so that no one can boast. It is a great advance for the One to grasp the benefits of grace and faith.

The Apostle Paul—enthusiast, mystic, theologian—bears the markings of a One. Introduced in the Book of Acts as one "breathing and threatening" destruction of the new sect of the Christians, this zealous Pharisee was all his life bent on righting the wrongs of the world. Following his dramatic conversion to the faith he had persecuted, he continued his crusading ways, a personality with a purpose, a choleric-melancholic bundle of focused energy.

As a One, St. Paul was logical: "For if the dead are not raised, then Christ has not been raised either. And if Christ has not been raised, your faith is futile" (1 Corinthians 15:16–17).

He was disciplined: "I beat my body and make it my slave" (1 Corinthians 9:27).

He had a keen conscience: "So I strive always to keep my conscience clear before God and man" (Acts 24:16).

He put principle and purpose ahead of comfort: "I have learned the secret of being content in any and every situation, whether well fed or hungry, whether living in plenty or in want" (Philippians 4:12).

He knew his imperfections: "Christ Jesus came into the world to save sinners—of whom I am the worst" (1 Timothy 1:15).

He liked to preach and teach: "So Paul stayed for a year and a half, teaching them the word of God" (Acts 18:11).

He came down hard on antinomians and slackers: "Shall we go on sinning so that grace may increase? By no means!" (Romans 6:1–2).

He was eager to vindicate himself before the bar of justice: "'I am now standing before Caesar's court, where I ought to be tried. . . . I appeal to Caesar'" (Acts 25:10–11).

He was not above getting in the last word: "Men, you should have taken my advice not to sail from Crete; then you would have spared yourselves this damage and loss" (Acts 27:21).

Throughout his life, Paul remained a morally serious person, mystically identified with his Savior, humbled by a "thorn in the flesh," and enraptured by the grace of God—and not his own works—in which he found all meaning and purpose.

Ones need to "ease up," "loosen up," "breath easy," and otherwise cultivate the art of relaxation, that they may leaven their lives with at least a measure of joy, as difficult as it may be for them to do so. For even in pursuit of leisure, they are likely to try too hard, to "strive" instead of to relax. They attempt to force the issue. Hence, there is a need to interrogate themselves, to challenge the super ego and its mistaken insistence that every moment be filled with vital activities.

They need, in fact, to be more objective toward themselves, surprising as that may sound to a supposedly objective type. For Ones fixate on principles that may or may not be true, yet that provide the stability they seek. Their logical abilities tend to come to the fore in defense of such principles; hence their talent at deductive reasoning, as alluded to above. Once given, the "truth," the "cause," the "method" is well defended by way of the One's logical rigor, but why that particular truth, cause or method was accepted in the first place is the object of a less careful consideration.

Despite its somber reputation, no book in the Bible besides Ecclesiastes better celebrates the deep but simple joys of everyday living, a message that Ones need to hear:

> • So I commend the enjoyment of life, because nothing is better for a man under the sun than to eat and drink and be glad (8:15).
> • A man can do nothing better than to eat and drink, and find satisfaction in his work. This ... is from the hand of God, for without him, who can eat or find enjoyment (2:24–25).
> • Light is sweet, and it pleases the eyes to see the sun. However many years a man may live, let him enjoy them all (11:7–8)

Ones are well advised to be thankful for that which is, not obsessed with that which might be. "Be joyful always; pray continually; give thanks in all circumstances, for this is God's will for you in Christ Jesus" (1 Thessalonians 5:16–18).

In addition, Ones need to curb their unhealthy and unbalanced attachment to life's rules and regulations. A sense of proportion is required. Rules and regulations, though good and helpful in themselves, can blind a person to weightier matters. This does not imply that a One should minimize concern for right and wrong. Rather, it recognizes that no amount of striving after obedience will, by itself, advance one's sanctification. No human performance "is ever good enough. There are always wrong desires in the heart, along with a lack of right ones, regardless of how correct one's outward motions are . . . and it is at the heart that God looks first."[9] When mindful of one's relationship to God, effort and resolve are commendable and profitable. Absent that relationship, they are ultimately hollow and futile.

Another concern is "the voice in the back of one's head." Conscience, that highly charged moral monitor, needs to be consulted with care, as it may be malformed, misinformed, or conditioned to place customary rules before essential rules. For the consciences of most are formed almost completely by family and community mores, which do not guarantee a perfectly attuned sense of right and wrong. Moreover, the conscience may be dulled or seared by repeated sins, in which case it clearly does not speak the wisdom of God. In opposition to the preceding, conscience needs to be imprinted with the code of an authentic revelation. Type Ones, especially, who tend to identify conscience with the voice of God, need to learn the distinction between the "weightier matters of the law" on the one hand, and scrupulosity on the other.

Additional areas of concern are a pronounced inclination to hold grudges and to brood on real or fancied slights. Ones erroneously think an offending party should know that he or she is in the wrong, hence confrontation with said party should be unnecessary if not unseemly. In such cases, the cold shoulder, the slow burn, the unspoken grievance take the place of confrontation and resolution. Better to face the object of one's ire and "clear the air," as suggested by William Blake:

> I was angry with my friend:
> I told my wrath, my wrath did end.
> I was angry with my foe;
> I told it not, my wrath did grow.

9. J. I. Packer, *Concise Theology*, 173.

In pursuit of integration, Ones need as much as possible to become "process persons." For they cannot, by force of will, order into being the circumstances they might wish. God determines the seasons; He has His timetable. He opens and closes doors, blocks and unblocks paths, makes smooth the road along which He wishes His subjects to travel. For the one secret of life and development "is not to devise and plan but to fall in with the forces at work—to do every moment's duty aright—that being the part in the process allotted to us: and let come—not what will, for there is no such thing—but what the eternal thought wills for each of us, has intended in each of us from the first."[10]

Striving in one's own strength achieves neither peace nor sanctity. Faith is required as well, and faith is a gift, not a product of striving. "Faith may result in action, and certainly true faith in Jesus always will result in action; but faith itself is not doing but receiving." [11] Imbued with faith, one is enabled to live and grow and act within the limits of what it means to be human. There is no longer the illusion of self-made perfection. Jesus alone, apart from the striving of type One, "is author and perfecter of our faith" (Hebrews 12:2).

This being said, Ones need to recollect the noble motive that lies at the base of all their striving and searching after the seemingly unobtainable, no matter how mistaken they may have been from time to time in navigating the shoals of life. For as more than one tradition teaches, "Truth is the ultimate goal of perfection: there is nothing beyond it and nothing this side of it but error; light springs from it; it is the soul of God."[12]

10. C.S. Lewis, quoting from *George MacDonald: An Anthology*, 134-135.
11. J. Gresham Machen, *What is Faith?* (The Banner of Truth Trust, Edinburgh, 1991), 89.
12. *The Golden Verses of Pythagoras*, 203–204.

5

Types and Triads

God ... so copied forth himself into the whole life and energy of man's soul, as that the lovely characters of Divinity may be most easily seen and read of all men within themselves.

~ John Smith the Platonist

THE HUMAN SPIRIT, or essence, is in contact with the Holy Spirit, or Divine Essence. This is so because human beings are theomorphic, that is, created in the image of God. As the Godhead itself is threefold or trinitarian, so too—as *Imago Dei*—are human beings threefold or trinitarian, as taught by St. Augustine and many others. As trinitarian beings, every person has spirit, soul and body. Moreover, every soul has reason, emotion and will, a "trinity within a trinity." The trinity of the soul and its importance to the enneagram is the main topic of this chapter, alongside the sub-topics of "intellect" and the subtle body.

To begin: if man is an *Imago Dei,* an image of God, of the One who is infinite in power, wisdom and goodness, whence his trials and troubles? According to sacred writ, such trials and troubles were not present to man's original nature. In the beginning, Creator and creature enjoyed an Edenic affinity. In the wake of the Fall, however, communion was sundered. Human beings, barred from the Tree of Life, became exiles from Essence.

Hence, to this day, men and women are bound to the "wheel of existence" (James 3:6, *New English Bible*). They are—as mapped on the wheel of the enneagram—captive to a nine-fold fixation. Cycles of rise and fall, gain and loss repeat themselves in each and every life. In the sardonic words of Ecclesiastes, "What has been will be again, what has been done will be done again; there is nothing new under the sun" (1:9). It is a world of disconsolation, relieved only by fleeting pleasures and limited achievements. It is ever revolving, ever recurring; a world of the coiled serpent, of the *ouroboros* biting its tail, of the closed circle, without exit. Individual egos are bound to the wheel, helpless in their own power to escape. They need both liberator and mediator, to free them from the wheel, to reopen the conduit between human and divine; to rebind, as it were, heaven and earth.

In speaking of the circular self-motion of the soul, Plato cast the soul itself—or an aspect of the soul—in the role of mediator, tied on the one hand to the ebb and flow of the psycho-physical domain and, on the other, to the immutable spiritual domain. Hence, the soul played a dual role, with the "ability to assimilate its activity to changeless truths as well as to things in a state of change."[1]

In Christian perspective, the soul's mediating function demands a supernatural mediator. The supernatural mediator, Jesus Christ, in obedience to the Father, died an atoning death for His people, commencing a liberation of souls, past, present and future, and a rebinding of soul to spirit. Moreover, as Scripture reveals, the Holy Spirit descended in fiery tongues on the disciples in the upper room, initiating a spiritual transmission that is the same yesterday, today, and forever. The Spirit is active in the "twice-born" human spirit, illuminating the soul, bringing balance, integration, peace, power and purpose.

The attainment of such a pleasing circumstance, however, is far from guaranteed. Though one be regenerated in one's spirit, one's soul—the seat of personality and the organ of consciousness—may be bound to the "wheel" in any number of ways. In attempting escape in its own strength, the soul pursues goals that render it ultimately unsatisfied. To attain its proper goal, it requires release from a host of impediments and destructive patterns, to allow the spirit to do its work. The psychological baggage of a lifetime, the burden of sins, bad choices, obsessions, compulsions, stresses and strains,

---

1. Robert Bolton, *Person, Soul, and Identity: A Neoplatonic Account of the Principle of Personality* (Minerva Press, London, 1994), 65–66.

must be addressed with insight and discipline. The life of sanctification has to be walked, even as God works by grace both within and
without, to bring deliverance. "The potter has in his mind's eye a
beautiful image which he would reproduce, and he molds it on the
wheel which is before him, and if it is yielding and plastic the result
is as he wishes. But if the clay is refractory, the vessel is marred—all
of which means that God will not do violence to the will of man."[2]

In this matter, the soul treats with God and no other. Ceremoni-
alism apart from knowledge does not suffice; the relationship needs
be personal, open, accepting. One's "clay" must be yielding not
refractory. There is no proxy religion; heart commitment is
required. "Self-realization through Christ is the end."[3]

Before turning to the soul and its faculties, some consideration
needs be given to the concepts of "intellect" and the subtle body.
Here, intellect is not to be identified with reason, which is limited to
natural mental functions. Rather, intellect is the conduit between
soul and spirit, as indicated in an earlier chapter. Its distinction from
reason is addressed by C.S. Lewis in *The Discarded Image,* wherein
he draws on Boethius, who wrote in the twilight of antiquity, and
Thomas Aquinas. According to Lewis, a clear line is distinguished
between *intelligentia* and *ratio,* with the former holding the superior
position. Moreover, *intellectus* is that in man which is closest to the
angelic *intelligentia,* the faculty that appropriates without exertion.
In other words, intellect allows the "simple . . . grasp of an intelligible truth, whereas reasoning . . . is the progression towards an intelligible truth by going from one understood . . . point to another. The
difference between them is thus like the difference between rest and
motion or between possession and acquisition."[4] One employs the
intellect when one simply "sees" a self-evident truth, as opposed to
the step-by-step procedures of reason. Intellect "sees" the certainties
embedded in essence or spirit. Such seeing is embryonic in all persons, engraved on their hearts but obscured by sin.

2. E.Y. Mullins, *The Axioms of Religion,* 90.
3. Ibid., 51.
4. *The Discarded Image: An Introduction to Medieval and Renaissance Literature* (Cambridge University Press, UK, 1998), 157.

Now, to the subtle body. In the same way that intellect is the immaterial link between soul and spirit, subtle body is the quasi-material link between soul and physical body. It is the soul's "subtle embodiment." Made of a fifth element or "quintessence," according to John Philoponus, it is a perpetual, non-temporal, non-decaying envelope or vehicle of the soul.[5] It is a sort of organizing principle, as well, making possible successive expressions of the same personality during the various stages of one's life, despite the ever-changing composition of the physical body. Moreover, following one's earthly span, it provides a vehicle, separable from the material body, for integration into one's spiritual archetype, therein to inhabit either paradise or *sheol*, heaven or hell.

Turning specifically to the soul itself, the enneagram—as we have seen—sets forth a nine-point typology in which healthy and unhealthy traits are described, analyzed and catalogued. The nine types are, in turn, placed within a trinity or triad of emotion, mind and will (or heart, head and belly), triads in which the special preoccupations and preferences—for good or ill—of the nine types can be analyzed.

The types in each triad (**see diagram 3**) share key elements of personality, as follows: The Two, Three and Four are in the Triad of the Emotions; the Five, Six and Seven, the Triad of the Mind, and the Eight, Nine and One, the Triad of the Will. This is not to say that the strengths and liabilities involving emotion, mind and will are isolated within these triads and found nowhere else, only that they are the predominating features of the types in their respective triads.

In dialectical fashion, the Triad of Emotion consists of types Two, Three and Four, with the Two over-expressing emotion, the Three most out of touch with emotion, and the Four under-expressing emotion. The Triad of the Mind consists of types Five, Six and Seven, with the Five over-expressing the ability to think, the Six most out of touch with thinking, and the Seven under-expressing thinking. The Triad of the Will consists of types Eight, Nine and One, with the Eight over-expressing volition, the Nine most out of touch with volition, and the One under-expressing volition.

5. Bolton, ibid., 220.

EMOTION
(Types 2, 3, 4)

REASON
(Types 5, 6, 7)

WILL
(Types 8, 9, 1)

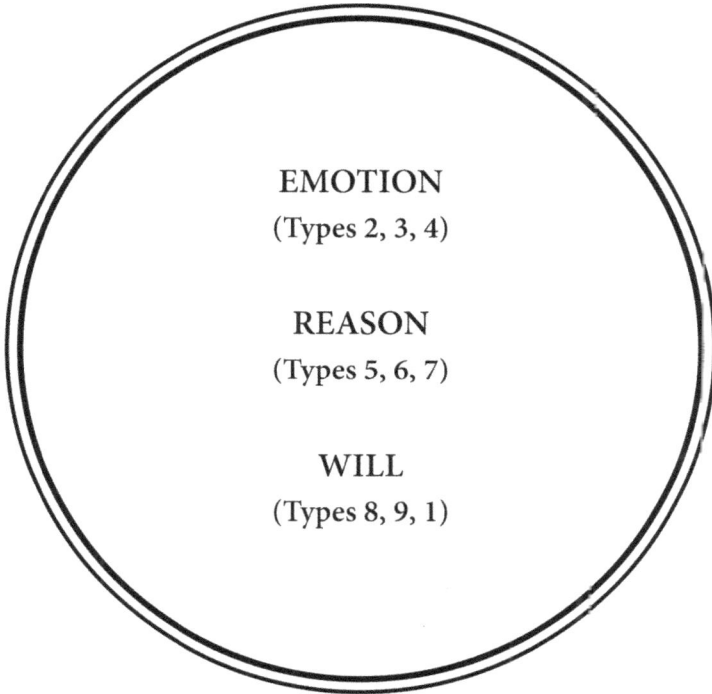

3. The Human Soul (psyche)

The unconscious (**see diagram 4**), the lowest realm of the subtle world, falls under the purview of soul. It is that aspect of soul that contains psychic material of which the conscious self is unaware. It is not, however, the be-all and end-all of psychological explanations, as taught by Freud and his epigoni and those who remain influenced by latter-day psychoanalytic trends.

This is not to deny the importance of the unconscious, for its forces do push people into emotional states and behaviors that conflict with their conscious wishes for internal peace and balanced relationships. One need not, however, remain passive before these forces; they can be addressed by prayer, introspection and counseling. For some, effective practices include Hesychasm (the prayer of the heart), meditation and dream work.

One must neither confuse or conflate the spirit with the unconscious. To do so is to acquiesce in a great modern inversion, in which the higher is interpreted in terms of the lower. This was among the errors of C.G. Jung: the reduction of the spiritual to "psychic contents." Moreover, owing to his clinical work, he focused largely on the mentally disturbed, confusing their dream imagery with the authentic symbolism devolving from the transcendent realm. Hence, he reduced transcendent realities to the "collective unconscious," a universal entity functioning *below* the conscious faculties of the soul, even while using it to account for the sacred symbols and archetypes that are above the soul.

According to René Guénon, the unconscious is better called the subconscious. "It happens that the subconscious, thanks to its contacts with psychic influences of the lowest order, effectively 'apes' the superconscious."[6] Thus, the lower counterfeits the higher, and the modern inversion continues apace. Such misleading ideas should not be allowed to shape an authentic spiritual teaching, nor should their confusions be allowed to adversely affect one's understanding of the enneagram.

---

6. *Symbols of Sacred Science* (trsl. by Henry D. Fohr, ed. by Samuel D. Fohr and James R. Wetmore (Ghent, NY: Sophia Perennis, 1995), 39.

SOUL

SUBCONSCIOUS

Lowest levels of the soul

Record of past emotions,
thoughts, motivations

Store of psychic wounds,
unhealed memories

BODY

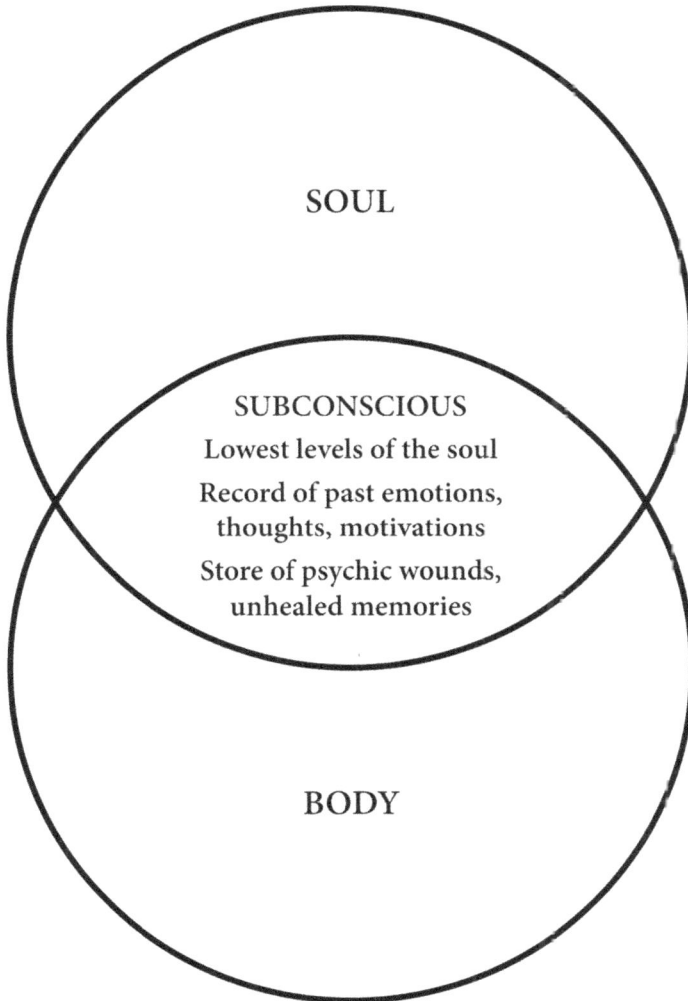

4. The Subconscious

6

Microcosm

There is an eternal vital correspondence between our blood and the sun. . . . We and the cosmos are one. The cosmos is a vast living body, of which we are still parts. The sun is a great heart whose tremors run through our smallest veins.
                                    ∼ D. H. Lawrence

T HE SOUL as microcosm, a notion present everywhere in traditional metaphysical teachings, has a contemporary counterpart in the "anthropic principle." This principle asserts that observation of the cosmos must be compatible with the conscious life that observes it.

Whatever else this principle may entail, it points at the very least to a link between the "starry skies above and the moral law within"— as a certain philosopher once put it — and thus mitigates against the idea that we are spiritual orphans amidst the meaningless immensities of space. Indeed, there would be no such perception possible if we did not possess a natural receptivity to the patterns and elements of the cosmos.

In traditional metaphysics, we are viewed as microcosms of all that is, seen and unseen. We are, in effect, little worlds within larger worlds; corporeal beings composed of cosmic elements, organic and inorganic, from the most subtle to the most solid. The elements of our body are no different from those of the animals: our lungs are adapted to the air we breathe, our eyes to light, our ears to sound; blood and lymph circulate within us as the stars circle about us; microscopic organisms thrive upon our substance; magnetic powers influence cellular activity. Whenever an object presents itself to our attention, it relates organically to our physical nature, be it the farthest sun or the nearest sunbeam, but not to physical nature only, but to soul and spirit as well.

In addition, then, to cosmological affinities, there are psycho-spiritual affinities between both human beings and supra-human beings. Owing to such links, it is the case that individuals and societies interact with the natural and supra-natural orders morally and spiritually in countless complex ways. The notion of the self as microcosm, then, implies there is nothing "out there" that is not "in here." The familiar Hermetic emblem, "as above, so below," clearly applies. This undermines the notion that human beings are essentially alienated from the context in which they exist, alive "in a world they didn't make," detached from larger worlds both within and without.

The forbidding vastness of the cosmos is no argument against affinities (or correspondences) between man, nature and supra-nature. Consider this image: a radiant summer sky and a group of simple folk gazing upon it.[1] These simple folk project upon the sky their dream of the hereafter. Now, suppose it were possible to transport them "into the dark and freezing abyss of the galaxies and nebulae." In this silent abyss, many of them "would lose their faith, and this is precisely what happens as a result of modern science, both to the learned and to the victims of popularization." What men and women of today do not know, however, is that this blue sky, "though illusory as an optical error and belied by the vision of interplanetary space, is nonetheless an adequate reflection of the Heaven of the Angels and the Blessed and that therefore, despite everything, it is this blue mirage, flecked with silver clouds, which is right and will have the final say."

To be surprised by this amounts to admitting that it is by chance that we are on the earth, that we see the earth and the sky as we do, that the "blue mirage" symbolizes what it does. But ... has not the Creator of all things, the fashioner of things seen and unseen— assuming we credit the reality of such a being—had wit enough to

1. Frithjof Schuon, *Understanding Islam* (World Wisdom Books, Inc., Bloomington, Indiana, 1998), 137–138.

arrange his symbols and his patterns of nature in such a way that they correspond to the patterns of the mind and spirit of his human creatures? Has he not, that is, made meaningful to them the cosmos in which he has placed them? This is not to say that the abyss of the galaxies does not reflect something in its own right, something besides the heaven of the angels. It reflects the terrors of the divine mysteries, too, "in which any man is lost who seeks to violate them by means of his fallible reason and without adequate motive." Either way, then, in both modern and archaic perspectives, one can discover a symbolic message.

The foregoing employs the method of a *scientia sacra,* a "sacred science," encompassing alike the faith of simple folk and the intellection of the educated. Sacred science largely concerns itself with the same objects as material science but looks at them differently, seeking to learn not only the physical attributes of these objects but the message they have for us. Sacred science concerns itself with the symbolism of appearances, with the "abysses of universal manifestation."

Such correspondences between man and nature find their larger context in the notion of the Great Chain of Being, an ancient view given a new name in the last century by Arthur O. Lovejoy, the historian of ideas. He called it the Principle of Plenitude, and used it to refer to the great, hierarchical chain of existents, arranged in an infinite number of links, from the most insignificant entities to the ones most proximate to Perfect Being, and with each link or "world" containing the principles of the worlds below it. The concept has been adapted by the contemporary thinker, Ken Wilbur, no stranger to enneagram theory. "According to the nearly universal view," he writes, "reality is a rich tapestry of interwoven levels, *reaching from matter to body to mind to soul to spirit.* Each senior level 'envelopes' or 'enfolds' its junior dimensions—a series of nests within nests of Being."[2]

The idea of the Great Chain of Being derives from the very ear-

2. *The Marriage of Sense and Soul* (Shambhala Publications, Boston, MA, 2001), 6–7.

liest times. It was clearly expressed first by Plato, then later and more fully by Plotinus and Proclus. Applied to the human microcosm, it says we correspond at various levels to the mineral, vegetable, animal, psychological and spiritual domains. On the plane of psyche, we find it echoed in the enneagram's "levels of development," as advanced by Don Richard Riso and Russ Hudson. This is not surprising, for traces of the Great Chain are detectable in one mode or another in all things psycho-spiritual and material.

Owing to these considerations, we follow the mathematician and philosopher Leibniz in his view that souls are "living mirrors or images of the universe of created things, but [that such] minds are also images of the Deity or Author of nature Himself, capable of knowing the system of the universe . . . each mind being like a small divinity in its own sphere."[3] This notion is reminiscent of the symbolism of the enneagram, itself a mirror of the soul, as well as the *Imago Dei*, the "image of God" in man.

According to the philosopher Robert Bolton, Leibniz's view was deeply influenced by Hermetic tradition, "which is distinguished as a meeting place of philosophy and magic, with its idea of reality which is microcosmic through and through."[4] Individual parts of the whole, he continues, "not only reflect the whole, but have powers of attraction and influence among themselves in proportion to . . . the ways in which they reflect the world and the degrees to which they do so. From thence come the evocative powers of magic and the influence of astrology."[5]

As indicated earlier, we believe the enneagram to be a microcosmic symbol, evoking "magical" relations between various planes of being. Indeed, we have long thought it represents a bit of "white magic." Does it not illustrate analogy and equilibrium between visible and invisible worlds, and can we not, by using it with discern-

3. Robert Bolton, *Self and Spirit,* quoting G.W.F. Leibniz, *The Monadology and Other Philosophical Writings,* Robert Latta, translator, Oxford: OUP, 1993, 83 (Sophia Perennis, Hillsdale, New York, 2005), 15.
4. Ibid.
5. Ibid.

ment, exert greater influence over our lives?[6] By using it to descend to our inmost selves, we come to view ourselves with a measure of objectivity. We attain a certain mastery over elements previously ungovernable. We find ourselves better equipped to achieve personal and transpersonal goals.

In all of this, we operate as a sphere of consciousness holding within itself a piece of the cosmos; an epitome or miniature of the larger organism in which we participate; the representative of a vital correspondence between that which is above, and that which is below.

6. Magic, Alain de Benoist says, is "a psycho-technique with a specific goal in mind . . . it constitutes the original 'know-how' of human self-domestication and the domestication of the psyche by consciousness." *On Being a Pagan* (ULTRA, Atlanta, Georgia, 2004), 22.

7

Rebirth

Rid the soul of illusions and passions and thus rid the world of a harmful being.
                                                    ~ Frithjof Schuon

"SECOND BIRTH" appears in a variety of forms in traditional doctrine. The Gospel's "born again" teaching is widely known in the West, but other religions and traditions offer variants of their own, both simple and complex. From the evangelical next door to the mystery devotee of ancient Greece, from the infant at the font to the *mystai* in the waves, those "born of water and spirit" are said to be heir to the kingdom of heaven.

Enneagram principles complement such spiritual forms by tracing the movement from soulish enneatype to liberated essence, demonstrating the paradox that we must, in some way, become different to become who we really are. We must transcend enneatype; transcend the psycho-physical being that has hitherto embodied our identity, and enter a fuller, more centered life, concentrated in the spiritual core or inner principle. Even then, however, and properly so, enneatype will retain its function as personality, as outward manifestation of the inner person, though partially relieved of former limitations and henceforth unified in the spiritual domain.

In the *Timaeus*, Plato described a similar dynamic (in which a man moves from a soulish to a spiritual state), touching on a great litany of key concepts, including mortal cravings, intellect, knowledge, wisdom, immortality, truth, divinity, happiness, original corruption, renewal and perfection.

> When a man is always occupied with the cravings of desire and ambition, and is eagerly striving to satisfy them, all his thoughts must be mortal, and, as far as it is possible altogether to become

such, he must be mortal every whit, because he has cherished his mortal part. But he who has been earnest in the love of knowledge and of true wisdom, and has exercised his intellect more than any other part of him, must have thoughts immortal and divine, if he attain truth, and in so far as human nature is capable of sharing in immortality, he must altogether be immortal; and since he is ever cherishing the divine power, and has the divinity within him in perfect order, he will be perfectly happy. Now there is only one way of taking care of things, and this is to give to each the food and motion which are natural to it. And the motions which are naturally akin to the divine principle within us are the thoughts and revolutions of the universe. These each man should follow, and correct the courses of the head which were corrupted at our birth, and by learning the harmonies and revolutions of the universe, should assimilate the thinking being to the thought, renewing his original nature, and having assimilated them should attain to that perfect life which the gods have set before mankind, both for the present and the future.[1]

These comments on human spirituality make room for both complex and simple souls alike, for intellectual sophisticates and uncultivated minds. Friedrich Nietzsche called Christianity "Platonism for the masses," and he was on to something, though perhaps not what he intended. For indeed the Christian religion is open to persons of all types and conditions, be they patrician or pleb, practical or visionary, and offers spiritual food to all who are in search of it.

Not Christianity only, but other faiths and traditions, also, despite disagreeing on exoteric matters, frequently agree on metaphysical themes of salvation and rebirth, sharing orthodoxy in the esoteric sense. Many of them define the natural human state as a kind of spiritual sleep. Persons are by nature "unawakened," subject to the

---

1. *Timaeus* 90, *The Dialogues of Plato,* translated by Benjamin Jowett (William Benton, publisher, Encyclopaedia Britannica, Inc. Chicago, 1952), 476.

ebb and flow of natural forces, with little or no understanding of their spiritual or transcendent nature. They are centered on *maya,* "illusion," or *samsara,* "wandering;" the passing world of ever-evolving, never arriving, ever-perplexing flux and change. "The greatest part of mankind . . . may be said to be asleep," writes William Law, "and that particular way of life which takes up each man's mind, thought, and actions may very well be called his particular dream."[2]

Yet owing to the intellect, and its link to spirit or essence, every person potentially experiences a core of transcendent certainties, independent of sensory experience, independent of the dream. Owing to this inner awareness, especially when cultivated by spiritual discipline and self-observation, there is discernment of the conflict between ego and essence, flesh and spirit, and the need for inner work to unify conflicting impulses. Of course, sensitivity to this tension varies from person to person. The one who remains in the dream is largely unaware of it. He is a man swimming downstream; he barely feels a thing. He gravitates to outward states corresponding to his inward inclinations; he "goes with the flow." The man swimming upstream is the one who feels the current. He is the awakened one, aligning his outward states to his progressively integrated certitudes, exercising a measure of independence from external forces.

As the enneagram makes clear, this is never easy. Swimming upstream never is. Moving "against the arrows"—to use the enneagram terminology for integration—never is. The shifting currents of the world beat against anyone who makes the effort; indeed, beat against him harder and longer than against the ones who capitulate to the currents. To move in the direction of integration, a person must employ volition and perseverance; a person must *will* to become who he or she really is. It is an inner and spiritual work, though never performed in one's own strength. The role of grace is fundamental; God's gift saves us from a "self-salvation" that is no real salvation at all.

2. *The Spiritual Athlete,* compiled and edited by Ray Berry quoting William Law from *The Spirit of Prayer* (Joshua Press, Olema, California, 1992), 286.

Rebirth—"second birth" or regeneration—opens up a world other than the one we customarily inhabit. For God calls to our inmost, spiritual core, to the "oldest" part in us, to the *Imago Dei* or *sensus divinitatis,* to "essence," to that spark or spirit that burns within us, and that burned also in the presence of the "Ancient of Days" (Daniel 7:9), in the time before time, in Christ himself, "before the foundation of the world" (Ephesians 1:4).

Rebirth opens possibilities transcending the psycho-physical domain. To varying degrees, it reestablishes the prerogatives that were ours in the first ages of humanity, before the race had fallen from its original estate, and during which—according to a hundred myths and legends—it experienced harmony with natural and supernatural entities, and served Divinity as vicegerent of the created order. The yearning for rebirth, the longing for "paradise lost," testifies to man's transcendent nature, and points to the futility of his attempts to satisfy such yearnings through profane pursuits alone, mere temporal attempts to recover timeless values. In enneagram language, rebirth is "integration into essence." It parallels on the psychological plane the transcendent operations of the spiritual plane.

Two additional thoughts come to mind regarding the move to essence: the importance of following a single religious path and the "praxis of the concordance." In recommending a single path, we do not advise on which path it should be. The theme of this book is metaphysical orthodoxy, a concept underlying every valid religious tradition. We argue neither the truth or error of these traditions, but leave such questions to the individual. This is not to say we do not affirm and practice one religious tradition ourselves, but to recognize that others may adhere to traditions other than our own. Our concern here is to urge the practice of a *single* tradition and to discourage syncretism.

To this end, we caution against performing the rites of two or more traditions. By combining rites, one perforce mingles disparate elements that are impossible to unify, despite esoteric parallels. In proportion to one's success in attracting miscellaneous spiritual influences, one introduces discordant psychic influences as well, sowing disorder and disequilibrium. "This situation," observes René

Guénon, "is similar to that of someone who, hoping to secure his health the more effectively, makes use at one and the same time of many different medicines the effects of which neutralize and destroy each other and sometimes even provoke unforeseen reactions harmful to his organism. There are things that are efficacious when used separately but that are nonetheless radically incompatible."[3]

The religious traditions are viewed as revelations by their followers; there is no revelation of a syncretistic religion, of a teaching that mixes a bit of Buddhism with a pinch of Christianity and a dollop of Islam. Rather, the religions are believed to have been imparted as wholes, as integrated *upayas,* as "packages" of consistent belief and practice. Hence the recommendation that one walk a single path, a path both deep and well marked by millennia of reflection and experience.

That being said, we draw attention to the esoteric principle of the "praxis of the concordance." Though practitioners of a single tradition, we do not advise living in a hermetically sealed vacuum, untouched by other traditions. It would be impossible to do so even if we wanted to. While adhering to one tradition, then, and while practicing its rites only, the praxis of the concordance (so named by Antoine Faivre)[4] encourages one to read, mark and study the various faiths, to illuminate similar themes between them, and to throw special light, from unexpected angles, on the teachings they present. In Faivre's words, this allows us "to establish common denominators between two different traditions or even ... among all traditions, in the hope of obtaining an illumination, a gnosis, of superior quality."[5]

To attempt mixed practice is dangerous; to learn from others is wisdom.

3. *Perspectives on Initiation* (Sophia Perennis, Ghent, New York 2001), 46.
4. *Access to Western Esotericism* (State University of New York Press, Albany, 1994), 14.
5. Ibid.

8

Effort and Grace

Grace is necessary to salvation, free will equally so—but grace in order to give salvation, free will in order to receive it. Therefore we should not attribute part of the good work to grace and part to free will; it is performed in its entirety by the common and inseparable action of both; entirely by grace, entirely by free will, but springing from the first in the second. ∼ Bernard of Clairvaux

F EELING, THINKING, AND WILLING, the three faculties of the soul, are the key elements of personality. Moreover, as indicated in the epigraph, free will and grace combine in a "common and inseparable" role. Owing to free will, we have power to direct our lives, subject to the influences of nature's laws and divine Providence, which provide the context in which the will is exercised.

Enneatypes Eight, Nine and One, members of the Triad of the Will, deal more directly with issues of free will, choice, self-activation and related matters than members of the other triads, but all nine types face them in one way or another. Free will, involving as it does the power to direct one's life, is a vital topic in discussing the enneagram. If one lacks the fundamental ability to choose, there is little reason to gain self-knowledge in the first place, little point in trying to balance one's personality or save one's soul.

This is not to say we are free agents in all matters, or that different persons exercise like amounts of volition. In broadest terms, as indicated above, we are governed in three ways: by Providence, by fate (nature), and by our choices. This ternary is discussed by Robert Bolton in his *Self and Spirit, Keys of Gnosis* and other writings.[1] We

1. This chapter owes much to Dr. Bolton's works. Though not a writer on the

Effort and Grace

are, he says, free to participate in either Providential or fatidic orders. The Providential order influences the spiritual or transcendent sphere; the fatidic determines the natural sphere, and the will determines our interactions with both Providential and fatidic spheres.

We do not choose to be Ones or Threes or Sevens; these personality patterns are etched in our psycho-physical natures by way of early experiences and genetic makeup, each of which is governed in turn by Providence. We can, however, exercise choice within these patterns, for they are less solidified than supple. The greater the exercise of choice, the greater our freedom over the constraints of the fatidic order.

Whence the power of choice, in a world of Providence and fate? It is a gift of God; God delegates causal power to created beings. Men and women, made in the image of God, share in God's attributes, with freedom of choice and rational capacity among them. As Plato observed, reason and order (attributed to the *Logos* in both pagan and Christian writings) are older than the material world, thus outside the realm of necessity. So too the power of choice, which maintains a measure of independence. Moreover, causality is cumulative; by exercising it, the person who chooses a specific course of action modifies his subsequent choices and the circumstances in which those choices are made. Hence, the exercise of choice widens the domain of personal freedom.

The relative importance of spiritual, psychological and physical energies waxes and wanes as each, in turn, receives attention from its human agent. In these relations, psycho-spiritual faculties compete with material faculties for available energy. Energy flows into various channels as attention shifts, either increasing or limiting one's power.

By directing energy toward transcendent values, one increasingly gains power—that is, a greater measure of freedom—over the material domain. In contrast, by directing energy toward material values, or refusing to choose in the first place, external causes become

enneagram, his views indirectly establish a metaphysic that serves as a foundation for it. Any failure to present his ideas clearly is the fault of the writer of this book.

determining factors. By abdicating responsibility, one gravitates to a set of outward conditions congenial to habitual preferences, that is, one follows the path of least resistance. The result is entropic drift, participation in *samsara* ("wandering"), acquiescence to the flux and flow of circumstance, as indicated earlier.

To curb one's bondage to material values, or one's unconscious acceptance of things as they are, one must not only exercise the power of choice but must activate the intellect as well. As explained elsewhere, activating the intellect is not the same as exercising one's powers of reason; it is, rather, yielding to transcendent values; it is acceptance of first principles, of the truths that prefigure and determine all other truths. It is to anchor oneself to immutable verities, to enter the domain of spiritual insight, thus, to gain release from psycho-physical bondage.

There's a catch however: one cannot do this by willpower alone. Volition is a faculty of the soul, like reason and emotion. Its power is limited. To enter the spiritual domain, through intellect, demands grace from God; demands, that is, a spiritual gift.

According to the aforementioned Robert Bolton, grace in this instance involves admitting "that we are not our own creators, so that what we achieve is to the honour of the Author of our being and not of ourselves alone. [Thus does a true understanding of grace humble the ego.] Our faculties as well as our being have also their own measure of dependence, since all the actions instigated by our wills require the co-operation of innumerable other forces within us and around us, most of which we know nothing about."[2] Our volition, then, acts consciously only on the tip of the iceberg, even as the vast mountain of cause and effect labors by necessity beneath our level of attention, however alert we might think ourselves to be.

Moreover, he continues, grace "expresses the law of Cosmic Sympathy by which like attracts like, in this case these being God and those who try to act according to God's will.... The fact that it is given freely is not the same as saying that it must be given to absolutely anyone; there must always be a correspondence between the receiver and the received, as in accordance with the law of Action

2. *Keys of Gnosis*, 125.

and Reaction."[3] The lifelong scoffer, then, lying on his deathbed with only minutes or hours remaining to him, displays little evidence of correspondence between himself and any grace that might come his way. He has chosen a thousand times to thwart the overtures of God; no "deathbed conversion" is likely to deliver such a seared and hardened soul.

By contrast, anyone who attempts spiritual disciplines in good faith finds grace at work in him, both to will and to do according "to God's good pleasure" (Philippians 2:12). Grace comes to him who believes; it does not come to the natural man, for grace is "foolishness to him" (1 Corinthians 2:14). The unredeemed ego admits of no escape from the circle of passions, because it is passion itself. Only the power of Another can supersede the power of the self.

According to the homely adage, God helps those who help themselves. Though not a direct saying of the Bible, it is nonetheless true. Self-activation and "God-activation" empower the will to exercise its freedom, to transmute individuals from soulish to spiritual beings, and to free them from the powers of personal and collective ignorance.

3. Ibid.

9

The Eye of the Heart

There is an eye of the soul which . . . is more precious far than ten thousand bodily eyes, for by it alone is truth seen. ～ Plato

"WITH THE EYES of your heart enlightened." These words are found in the writings of St. Paul (Ephesians 1:18)), but not there only. They are well-nigh universal, present alike in East and West. They cast light, as it were, on the distinction between essence and psyche, a subject discussed at some length earlier, even as they introduce an idea of universal significance.

By their allusions to sight, to light, and to the heart, they recall both present-day and traditional meanings. For either seeing or not seeing, metaphorically speaking, are freighted with significance. Light corresponds to knowledge; darkness, to ignorance. We speak of "seeing the light," of having a "flash of genius," of a light bulb going on over one's head. Or we say that someone is "blind to the truth," that another is "in the dark," or that "the blind are leading the blind." St. Paul's phrase, mentioned above, has a less everyday meaning to it, pertaining instead to a dimension above or beyond our tangible, physical senses. These inner eyes open on the essence (or spirit) both within us and without.

As intimated above, this symbolism is present in many places and in many ages. Elsewhere in the West, it is found in St. Augustine as the eye of divine Wisdom, illuminating the human mind. It is found in the words of Jesus, also, in the eighth beatitude, where he says the pure in *heart* shall *see* God. Sufi Muslims have long used the phrase, as did sages in the twilight of antiquity. For their part, Hindus call it the "third eye," the "eye of Shiva," the spiritual eye that sees eternity, as opposed to the corporeal eyes that see physical phenomena only.

The Eye of the Heart

One can find it among the native Americans. Listen to a wise man of the Lakota:

> I am blind and I do not see the things of this world; but when the Light comes from On High, it illuminates my heart and I can see, because the Eye of the heart sees all things. The heart is the sanctuary at the center of which is a small space where the Great Spirit lives, and this is the Eye of the Great Spirit by which He sees everything, and with which we see Him. When the heart is impure [shades here of Jesus and his beatitude], the Great Spirit cannot be seen.... To know the Center of the Heart where the Great Spirit dwells, you must be pure and good and live according to the way that the Great Spirit has taught us. The man who is pure in this way, contains the Universe in the Pocket of his Heart.[1]

These are the words of "one who knows," a Jesus or a St. Paul of the Great Plains. Like the Bible, he teaches a traditional view, in which people are seen not only as physical and psychological beings but as spiritual beings, linked not only to their own thoughts and feelings and actions, but to a transcendent or spiritual plane. "The man who is pure ... contains the Universe in the Pocket of his heart." When human beings are pure, unified in their heart of hearts, so to speak, with the spiritual dimension of life, they "see" God; they "see" the Great Spirit.

These cross-cultural references are at one in drawing attention to the widespread importance of the inner eye, or "inner eyes." Traditionally, human beings have always and everywhere paired inner seeing and illumination with the heart, with the center or—in enneagram vocabulary—the essence of what it is to be human. As mentioned earlier, Jesus taught that the pure in heart would see God. He taught this as a beatitude, as a state of being that made one blessed or happy. Such happiness he promised to those whose deepest self was pure, that is, whose deepest self was unmixed in motive,

---

1. Frithjof Schuon, *The Eye of the Heart* (World Wisdom Books, Bloomington, Indiana, 1997), 9. The quotation is from Black Elk, priest and holy man of the Oglala Sioux.

free from division, single-minded, undiluted by anything devious, ulterior, hypocritical, base, deceitful. Without guile. In short, utterly sincere. Such lives are transparent before God and man. Such a state makes God visible to the eyes of faith in the here and now, and to the eyes of eternity in the hereafter.

It is in the direction of this state that the enneagram points, as one peels away the layers of psychological baggage that have accumulated during one's lifetime. As one continues the "peeling," fresh aspects of essence begin to emerge, and healthy aspects of the psyche as well. Elements of a transmuting self become visible, owing to the enhanced perception of the inner eyes.

As noted, it was in St. Paul's letter to the Ephesians that he speaks of the eyes of the heart. Ephesus was a pagan city, Greek and Roman, though some Jews lived there and Christians had founded a church, consisting of both Jews and Gentiles. To fully understand their calling, Paul said the Father must enlighten the "eyes of their hearts." They were not to "enlighten themselves" but to *be* enlightened, to receive a spirit of wisdom and revelation. It was to be a gift, a grace, from God. A gift of wisdom, the power to discern and judge things rightly; a gift of revelation, the ability to understand what God had made known. With the eyes of their hearts enlightened, they would learn of the riches of their spiritual inheritance.

Paul knew the Ephesians were impure; they were flawed, limited, less-than perfect beings, like everyone else. They could not lift themselves by their sandal straps, so to speak. Enlightenment was a gift. God bestowed it on those who prayed and those who were prayed for, and, even then, it didn't arrive overnight. It took time. As Paul wrote, it would only happen "as you come to know him," that is, to know God.

We live in a pragmatic, results-oriented culture; we want things to happen now, if not yesterday. Speed is of the essence (no pun intended). We lack patience. If we want a book, we turn on the computer, we type in some words, a couple of clicks later, we've ordered the book and it's in the mail. In the spiritual domain, however, things are less immediate. One cannot open the eyes of the heart on command, for the light of God is at first too bright to gaze upon without a measure of time for adjustment. It is like walking into the noonday sun from a darkened movie theatre, or driving out of a tunnel into a blaze of light. Or, to change the metaphor, it's like the tilling of soil, the planting of seeds, the watering of the ground, then, and only then, will the light of the midday sun bring forth, success- fully, a thriving plant from its place of burial.

Considered from another angle, getting to *see* the light, getting to *know* God, is something like getting to know another person. In fact, it *is* getting to know another Person, especially in the Western faiths, but here and there in the East as well; in bhakti yoga, for example, or, even more so, in Amitabha Buddhism, with its doctrine of salvation by faith. Like getting to know another person, it takes time, it takes adjustment. One gets a better picture of the person as time goes by, as the eyes adjust and see both the bright spots and the shadows. One sizes up the other person with the outer eyes (and ears) initially, from what one sees and hears; in time, the eyes of the heart, the inner eyes, are brought into play. A deeper kind of seeing, a deeper kind of knowing, begins. We come to know God in our hearts, to know with increasing certainty the things he has planned for those who love him. Such things, Paul proclaimed, as the riches of his spiritual inheritance among the saints, and the greatness of his power for those who believe; the things that do not darken but lighten the everyday lives we live. These are things Paul wanted the Ephesians to know and understand; this is why he wanted the eyes of their hearts enlightened. This is why we, too, are urged to see through new eyes, through the eyes of the heart.

It is these spiritual eyes that discern not only transcendent reali- ties, but the psychological realities within us as well. Spiritual eyes are able to "stand back" and observe the dynamics of the psyche; its "type-related" behaviors, its evasions and shortcomings. There are no "ten easy steps" to obtain this capacity, no simple formula, no sure-fire technique. Only by meditation on the Word; by prayer; by self-knowledge; only in these does one experience the deeper dimensions of seeing, the way of seeing that comes as a gift, but a gift that can be sought and asked for. We cannot have it on demand, it likely will not come in a flash of lightning. "This thing," the Sufis say, ". . . can never be found by seeking, yet only seekers find it." We *can* prepare for it, that is all. When it does come, it will come intermittently, just a moment or two, now and then. It will come as Spirit comes: "The wind blows where it wishes, and you hear its sound, but you do not know where it comes from or where it goes. So it is with everyone who is born of the Spirit" (John 3:8).

Once the eyes of the heart—the eyes of faith and knowledge, the eyes of the spirit—have been opened, no matter how briefly and intermittently, one begins to live in two worlds, the one supra-temporal and the other temporal; the one "in the heavens," the other, on earth. One lives *in* the world but is not *of* the world. It is the unification of Being with becoming. One sees through new eyes, and brightness comes, bit by bit, even as a root develops a stalk and branches and leaves and buds and flowers, and reaches after the sunlight.

10

Integration
and Disintegration

Transmutation is a great mystery, which is by no means—as fools
suppose—contrary to the course of Nature, or the law of God.

⟶ Paracelsus

OD'S SPIRIT, working through the human spirit, has ample
access to the balanced, permeable soul. By contrast, God's
Spirit, working through the rigidified, compulsive ego, has
little access to the soul. Ego reduction—the taming of the ego—
needs to make "soul space" in which the Spirit can work.

As a form of spiritual alchemy, the enneagram serves just this
purpose. In doing so, it finds its place among the "sacred sciences,"
among those disciplines that aim to recognize man's role as a microcosm within the macrocosm, as a miniature world within a larger
world, and to address his needs accordingly. As we saw earlier, the
purpose of sacred science is fundamentally different from the purpose of empirical science. While the latter gathers facts and pro-
poses theories regarding the natural world, even while treating that
world by and large as an infinitely complex but soulless mechanism,
sacred science aims at finding a "message" or "meaning" in the natural world, especially in regard to demonstrating or preserving individual and cosmic balance. This is clearly true of operative alchemy
and, by extension, of spiritual alchemy.

Alchemy's first principle is *solve et coagula,* that is, dissolution or
separation of "chaotic" and "primal" matter into its constituent elements, after which it is reassembled or "coagulated" in a new
arrangement. In the work of the enneagram, this translates into the
analysis, exposure and neutralization of the rigidified and compul-

sive elements of the ego, followed by their reassembly on a higher plane. In exoteric terms, this is the "sanctification" of which the theologians speak, in which the believer grows in grace by way of alternating spiritual deaths and resurrections. In each case, the soul progresses through many levels or states of being before attaining its final end.

Transmutation, then, is a process subtle and complex, involving the integration of the scattered, discordant elements of the ego into an increasingly harmonious whole, centered within a transcendent, guiding principle. As the return to Eden is blocked, and full ascent to the Absolute awaits the hereafter, transmutation does not reach completion in the here and now. Nevertheless, a sense of greater spiritual and psychological awareness, of greater openness and integration, awaits those who reduce the ego to make room for spiritual illumination.

In moving beyond the prison of egocentrism, then, aspirants develop a sense of balance, of lightness, of freedom, thus liberating potentials that have been pressing for release. Conversely, those on the path of disintegration experience a hardening of the ego. Disconsolations continue to depress and distort the personality; spirit remains encrusted and confined.

Paradoxically, the enneatype lying in one's direction of *disintegration* embodies the very aspects of personality most needed *for* integration.[1] Yet the ego, according to Riso and Hudson, is not yet able to manage those aspects of personality; until it can do so, integration will fail. For example, the One most needs to deal with self-inhibition, symbolized by Four. To deal with self-inhibition, however, the One must first move in the direction of Seven, to its point of *integration,* where it will assimilate a measure of the Seven's unbounded sense of adventure, affirmation of pleasure, and all-around delight in life—a reduction of self-inhibition, indeed. It is necessary, then, to move first "against the arrow" to the point where the ego's unhealthy habits can be addressed directly. This is a daunting prospect. It means facing aspects of the personality—

1. See Don Richard Riso and Russ Hudson, *Personality Types: Using the Enneagram for Self-Discovery* (Houghton-Mifflin Company, New York, 1996), 415.

the Jungian "shadow" as it were—that have been hidden and suppressed.

It is also the path to a freer, more balanced inner life. It is the
means of slaying or neutralizing habitual sins and hampering behaviors that have fed the ego and blocked the workings of the Spirit. As
one creates inner space in which the Spirit can work, one actualizes
one's rebirth by way of "sanctification," by transmutation of lead
into gold.

PERSONAL relationships are primary to the Two, and the helping of
others the main source of self-worth. Twos, who over-express feeling, do not need to be told more than once that "It is more blessed
to give than to receive." They gain a sense of superiority by helping
others; they try to be all things to all people. "Lean on me" could be
their motto, as they attempt to play the part of a benevolent deity.

When Twos become unbalanced, they follow the arrow (**see diagrams 5 and 6 for directions of disintegration and integration of
the types**) to the Eight, where they take on the unhappy features of
that formidable type. They may seek vengeance against a significant
figure in their life, someone who has spurned them or shown ingrat-
itude. They become aggressive and manipulative and anger rises to
the surface. Their mission in life, to be loved and valued for the
things they do, has failed, and they have come full circle, expressing
hatred instead of love.

When Twos move toward wholeness and balance, they work
against the arrow to take on the healthy attitudes of the Four. They
no longer need to live by way of self-publicized altruism, gaining
a sense of worth as helpers and saviors. Like a healthy Four, they
begin to look inside, to become aware of their emotions. At last, they
are able to admit their needs, faults, pains and motivations. Pride
is unveiled and curbed. Twos are enabled to open up to others,
to reveal themselves. They even learn to ask for help. They realize
that love and care *from* others equips them to provide enhanced love
and care *to* others. They learn true humility, to accept the perspective of Luke 17:10, where the diligent servants admit, "We are unworthy . . . we have only done our duty."

The Three must always appear competent, in control, successful.

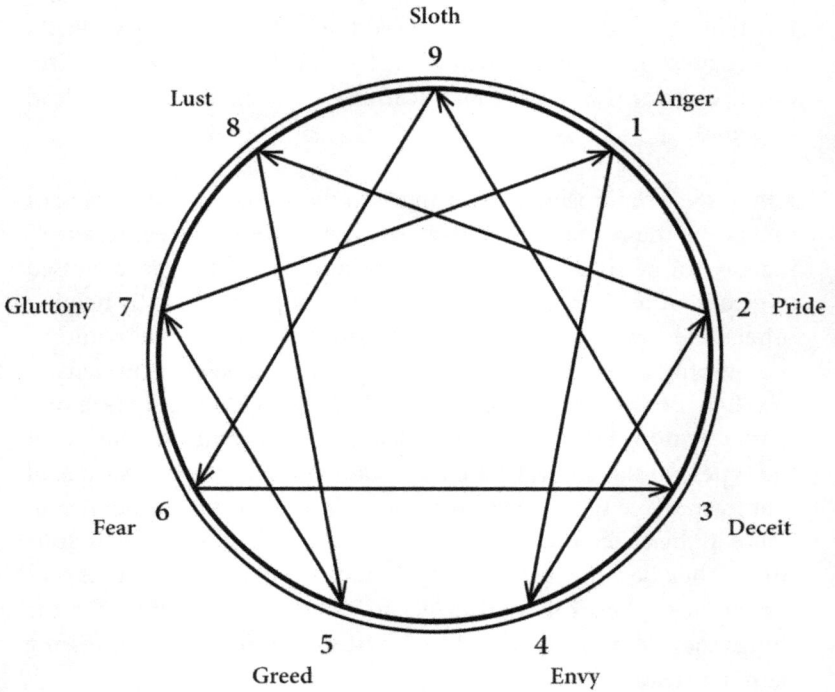

5. Directions of Disintegration
and Passions

Integration and Disintegration

In short, number Three, who is most out of touch with feeling, intends to be "number one." In carrying out this program, Threes fall in love with their image, the image they have themselves created and cultivated in conformity with the dictates of the surrounding milieu, while ignoring their inner self. At the same time, they look at others in terms of their importance and usefulness to the Three's own ends. Despite the cool and competent persona, they experience plenty of psychic strain as they cover up their real selves, keeping others—and themselves—at a distance from inner doubts and weaknesses. In this, they deceive first themselves, then others.

When Threes disintegrate, they follow the arrow to Nine and, like an unhealthy Nine, see life as no longer worth the effort. As they experience growing frustration with failure, they become hostile to others in word and deed, experiencing little or no guilt as they do so. In short, they tune out their feelings, even more than usual. The energetic, competent and efficient aspects that define them when healthy are lost.

When Threes integrate by moving against the arrow, they take on the best qualities of the Six. As we have seen, Threes tend to rank personal success as priority number one, and use others as means to their ends. Not so the Six, who is loyal to the group and faithful in relationships. By integrating in this direction, Threes become aware of their feelings and of the tug of conscience, becoming more cooperative and concerned for the welfare of others. Growing awareness of the inner self develops. They admit their weaknesses and the need for "something more" than mere image and competence. They begin to cultivate others for their own sake, no longer as means to egocentric ends. Best of all, they reach a point where they are, quite simply, honest . . . even when no one is looking.

The Four is "an artist of life," bringing to the canvas of everyday existence a sensibility that is not everyday. To the Four, the past—romantic and distant—and the future—filled with alluring visions—bear the most significance, not the moment at hand. In addition to flights of imagination, the Four—who under-expresses feeling—engages in a sophisticated presentation of the self, esteeming the self as something special, as something finer, than the self of others. Fours are actors, not in scene-setting alone but in sensitivity and

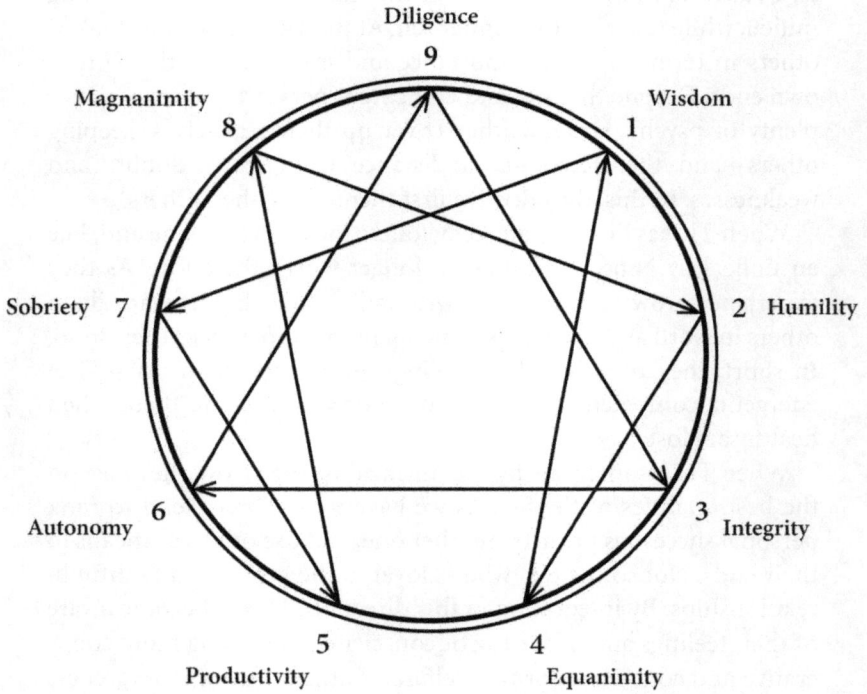

Diligence
9

Magnanimity
8

Wisdom
1

Sobriety 7

2 Humility

Autonomy 6

3 Integrity

5
Productivity

4
Equanimity

6. Directions of Integration
and Virtues

emotional richness. They are subject to excitable feelings that buffet them across a spectrum of moods, from depression to elation. Hesitant to join the crowd in its pedestrian pursuits, they find themselves isolated, unfulfilled and unaccomplished, despite talent and promise, and feeling defective and depressed.

When they disintegrate, they follow the arrow to Two. There they become dependent, cleaving to others for support. Hence, they develop an unhealthy reliance on the other as caregiver. Moreover, they become aware they have let the years roll by, that their dreams have not been realized. This hurts their self-image, for (like Twos) they crave the admiration of others. At low ebb, they spiral out of control, overwhelmed by negative feelings.

By moving against the arrow, Fours take on the healthy habits of the One. They learn to discipline themselves, to press themselves on the environment. They take themselves in hand, reason with themselves, move into action. They seek achievement and identify objective values. No longer pushed and pulled and stymied by feelings, they put their gifts to work. They move beyond introversion and subjectivity, yet express the richness of their interiority. They become special in the healthy sense of the word.

To the Five, to the type that over-expresses thinking, "to know is to be." Fives are natural ascetics, contemplatives, gnostics. Their real world is the mind, thus they are detached, private, interior beings. They fear envelopment by the world and by others; they fear losing their identity, they fear losing a bit of themselves if they give too much to others. They hoard time, emotions, thoughts and possessions as means to preserve autonomy against a threatening world.

Deteriorating Fives follow the arrow to Seven, where they become impulsive, irrational, and detached from practical application of their mental gifts. Like Sevens, they avoid the unpleasant aspects of life, allowing fantasies and disordered thoughts to dominate. Such developments are coupled with paranoia, isolation and restless action, traits of the unhealthy Seven, and fear becomes an ever-present reality.

When they integrate, they move against the arrow to Eight. Eights instinctively press themselves against the world, modeling an assertiveness the Five needs to emulate. By learning to channel their turbulent minds in creative ways, they discharge their thoughts in purposeful action, putting into practice their great store of theory and knowledge. Even if they do not know everything about a subject, they are ready to stand up and be counted. As a result, fear diminishes.

Compliant, ambivalent and overly serious, Sixes—who are most out of touch with thinking—are both fearful and aware of being fearful. Perceiving the world as threatening, they build barriers of psychic protection. They shy away from new ideas, preferring the tried and the true, the established tradition that can be relied on in a world of ebb and flow. Unable to trust themselves, they look to the Pope, the firm, the party or some other authority to give them the assurance they need. Frightened and tentative on their own, they brim with confidence when their cause is sanctioned by authority. Though generally phobic, they can be counter phobic as well, acting out of character and defying the fears that prey on them.

Unhealthy Sixes follow the arrow to Three, where they become hyperactive, aggressive and insecure, seeking their ends with bluster and intimidation. In defying their fears and ambivalences, they pursue success at any cost. They become violent in trying to conceal their fears and felt inferiorities. They act out against those whom they believe have persecuted them.

The Six makes peace by moving against the arrow into the space of the self-accepting Nine. Inner conflicts ease and reconciliation of impulses becomes possible. Sixes become less anxious about what the group thinks; peace and harmony become important values. At the same time, they become more trusting of divine intentions. They learn to "die" in order to "live," countering ingrained prejudices with spiritual wisdom. Even in the absence of guaranteed security, they venture into the unknown. They become inwardly stable, less fearful, more trusting of others.

Optimistic seekers of perpetual happiness, Sevens—who under-express thinking—avert their gaze when trials and unpleasant truths come their way. They follow the gospel of bliss, amidst a whirl of pleasures, multiple options and frivolous entertainments. At their worst, they are like spoiled children, demanding instant gratification, overindulging the senses and taking no responsibility toward the unhappier aspects of life. On the positive side, they are likeable and sometimes irresistible. They are quick learners, jovial companions and engaging conversationalists. Yet deep in the psyche is a nagging dread of meaninglessness and extinction, of an end to the never-ending party. On account of this, they run faster and faster, afraid to look back, afraid a menacing reality will catch up to them if they stop to catch their breath.

Sevens disintegrate along the path to One, as they attempt to introduce a semblance of order into their manic behavior. In doing so, they become, like unhealthy Ones, aggressive and punitive, for they resent the limits they impose on themselves and become rebellious, leading to further outrageous behavior and continuing deterioration. More generally, they resent losing the hope of a trouble-free life, owing to their excesses and unrealistic expectations.

Sevens attain balance with a move to Five. Working against the arrow, they slow their pace and become more observant of themselves and others, learn to avail themselves of reason and moderation, and become aware of the Transcendent ("Be still and know that I am God"). Moreover, they learn the trials they face are a means of growing in the spiritual life, and that "Whom the Lord loveth he chasteneth." Holiness eclipses superficial happiness, and they realize trials are "only for a season." By looking at the world in greater depth, they begin to savor the pleasures of life with gratitude.

Eights—who over-express the will—are "bigger than the world," instinctive and powerful, natural leaders. Choleric, energetic, intimidating, characterized by all-or-nothing thinking, they exercise control and play power games. They dismiss the authority of others, be that authority political, legal, moral or medical. Uncanny at ferreting out the weaknesses of others, they are cunning in hiding their own ("Never let the other guy see you sweat"). Despite a lust for domination, they seek to redress injustices, bearing within themselves a soft spot for the weak and the underdog.

When they follow the arrow to Five, Eights begin to fear for survival. The people on whom they have trampled are potential avengers, ready to strike the one who has dominated them. They become paranoid, like an unhealthy Five. Also, like a Five, they withdraw from action—normally their chosen domain—and keep watch on things from a distance. Henceforth, they are defined by suspicion, delusion, isolation, and vulnerability to total defeat.

When Eights move against the arrow toward the Two, they place their instinctive energy on the side of their better angels. Already drawn to the underdog in their healthier moments, they now move in a principled manner to come to the aid of those in need. Moreover, their aggressiveness is tempered by empathy for the needs and feelings of others in general. In addition, they "open up" and let others see beneath their armor, allowing a glimpse of vulnerability. To show honest emotion is a risk but, also, an opening to others.

Nines—who are most out of touch with the will—seek unity and tranquility. When healthy, they are stable, supportive, optimistic; they excel at peacemaking. Everyone wants them around, for they are down-to-earth, friendly, genuinely nice. But when unhealthy, they slip into indifference and neglect, failing to order and discipline their lives. Their progress in self-development is slow and spotty, hampered by inertia. They are prone to regression, sliding back to homeostasis. Their personalities become bland, "neither hot nor cold." Afraid to set priorities, they tread the backwaters of life . . . and the strong, main currents pass them by.

Disintegrating Nines follow the arrow to Six. In despair over lack of achievement, they are beset by anxiety, like a fearful Six. Normally placid, they strike out at others, even as they remain dependent on them. They become self-punishing, and find themselves filled with doubts about their course in life. They doubt the intentions of others, too, reacting like an angry Six—sometimes violently—toward those who seek to nudge them into action.

The integrating Nine moves against the arrow by taking on the healthy qualities of the Three. Nines at this point become more assertive, exchanging their tendency to withdraw from life in favor of participation. They learn to set goals and to strive for their fulfillment. They develop a sense of self-worth; healthy emotions break through. They stop being ciphers. They take charge of their lives and develop independence and optimism, confidant their quest for unity will find its place in the everyday activities of life.

Ones—who under-express the will—seek order, decency, and a clear conscience. They see the world as black and white; they despise ambiguity. Above all, they seek rectitude; they strive to be right about things large and small. They are good and dutiful people, interested in fair play and proper conduct. Yet the harder they try, the more active the inner devils become, pricking their conscience with obsessive guilt. They come to view life as a series of tasks that defy completion. Like Sisyphus, they reach the top of the mountain, only to see the stone roll back down the slope. They never reach the goal, complete the chore, or master the subject in keeping with the standards they set. In their view, the good is always the enemy of the best. For being finite and imperfect—for being, in a word, human— they judge themselves harshly.

When Ones follow the arrow to Four, they collapse beneath self-imposed burdens. They become depressed, suffering dramatically like a melancholy Four. The perfect has eluded them and they give up, sinking into anger and despair. They feel guilty about their shortcomings, and distressed about the narrow-minded state into which they have fallen. Their hypocrisies become more apparent, even as they condemn others with self-righteous zeal.

Ones attain balance by integrating to Seven. At Seven, they find optimism, a sense of fun, a break with routine. Ones at Seven take life and themselves a little less seriously. By integrating as they do, they stop resenting the world's imperfections. They strive less but achieve more. They learn that virtue is its own reward and brood less on the weaknesses of others. They become valued for the guidance they give, becoming figures of wisdom. Indeed, they become "wise as serpents but gentle as doves."

11

Transmutation
or Transformation?

Thus we never find a vein of lead, for instance, which does not contain a few permanent grains, at least, of gold and silver.
~ Nicholas Flamel

I T HAS BEEN COMMON, if not universal, for enneagram teachers and theorists to speak of "transformation" rather than "transmutation" as the goal of enneagram work. We too have done this in past writings, to preserve the vocabulary that has been used and to reflect the typical usage one finds in psychological terminology and daily speech. Despite accepted practice, it seems to us that using transformation for this purpose is misleading, though not surprising. Indeed, one finds similar overlaps and confusions in dictionary definitions. Such ambiguity renders an important concept rather muddled and, consequently, lacking in the rigor that should attach to it. Hence, we use the word transmute, as more accurately expressing the process we have in mind.

A little background might make our purpose clear. When one speaks of transformation etymologically, one speaks of a "passage beyond form." The "form" under discussion is the body, not the psyche or the spirit, which are non-corporeal and thus without form. For its part, a transformed body is freed from the corporeal restrictions of everyday existence.

Transformation of the latter kind, for example, was the intent of the Eleusinian Mysteries of the ancient world, specifically in the Greater Mysteries, which aimed to evoke mystical visions of happiness of soul both here and hereafter. The goal was to purify the initiate of the "defilements" of material nature and to obtain for him a new form—a new and differently constituted body—in which to be elevated to spiritual vision. Thus elevated, he would, it was believed, enjoy the primordial, supra-individual principles from which the race had originally descended. In the New Testament, a parallel is found in the Resurrection, in the form of a "glorified body," in both the person of Jesus and as a promise to his followers.[1] In transformation, then, the body itself is changed, allowing it to partake of supra-temporal realities, beyond duration and perpetuity.

By contrast, transmutation—a central concept in alchemy, both operational and spiritual—was applied to the Lesser Mysteries. In these, the aim was a change not *of,* but *within,* the formal domain, including the totality of individual states present in soul and spirit. Transmutation involved mostly the psychological domain, thus the faculties of soul addressed by the enneagram. We say "mostly," for psychological integration overlaps with integration into essence or spirit, even when analysis begins with psyche or soul.

In a related vein, astonishing as it sounds, higher states of psychological integration may allow an individual in rare cases to attain a supra-individual condition, even as he or she continues to inhabit a terrestrial setting. In such a state, according to René Guénon, "the very elements that make up the body can be 'transmuted' and 'subtilized' so as to be transferred to an extra-corporeal modality, where the being can thenceforth exist in conditions that are less narrowly limited than those of the corporeal domain, particularly in respect of duration." In this connection, he claims that the *Siddhas* of India "exist in the extra-corporeal prolongations of the human domain,"[2] a perfected state including paranormal abilities. We would also point out the miracles of Christian saints, ranging from levitation

---

1. In the Gospel accounts of Jesus after the Resurrection, we are told that he appeared "in another form" but that he could be seen, heard and touched. Moreover, he was several times not recognized at first sight, appeared and disappeared in uncanny ways, and even ate broiled fish. His was the prototype of the resurrected or glorified body.

2. *Perspectives on Initiation,* translated by Henry D. Fohr (Sophia Perennis, Ghent, New York, 2001), 266.

and prolonged fasts to bilocation and incorruptibility.[3] This being said, such phenomena are rare and we suspect excite little interest—and perhaps a great deal of skepticism—among adherents of the enneagram, unless they happen to aspire to sainthood(!) or wish to pursue elevated states of consciousness, endeavors that would take them far beyond any ordinary use of the system.

For the above reasons, it is our opinion that transmutation, not transformation, is the most accurate term to use when discussing the integrated states of being that can be attained by use of the enneagram.

3. Of course, such phenomena are dismissed by secular thinkers and even many religious believers, and fraudulent incidents of this kind are all too well known. Even so, the metaphysical possibility cannot be dismissed, and the witness of the ages is not unfavorable.

12

Freedom and Power

Thou shouldst know that it is inner abandonment that leads men to the highest truth.
～ Henry Suso

A MONG THE GOODS of life, we seek few things more ardently than personal freedom and the power to establish that freedom. Freedom and power: touchstones of longing and imagination. If only, for example, we were free of irritating acquaintances, or of demanding superiors, or of limited financial resources, or of nagging habits, or of imperfect health, or of a dead-end occupation, or . . .

Or . . . of this, that, or the other thing. Insert whatever "if only" we prefer, we are convinced that its removal would make life a great deal more livable, perhaps even usher in our own little paradise.

But, where shall we find the power to attain such freedom? If by great good fortune we have discovered the enneagram, we might apply *it* to the attainment of such goods. By coming to know in depth and detail our enneatype, and by applying such knowledge to the pressure points of life, we might succeed in achieving all or some of the aforementioned goods, and others besides.

Voila! A "technology of success."

By thus applying the enneagram to our condition, we could pursue the ends that move the minds and hearts of many of our contemporaries, and more than not ourselves as well. That the enneagram can be put to such ends testifies to its near-universal applicability. Enneagram pioneer G.I. Gurdjieff claimed, after all, that every process could be mapped upon it. Moreover, there is nothing wrong in pursuing such ends, for we are not "angels"—spirits without bodies —but composite creatures of body, soul and spirit, thus linked to a spectrum of goods touching on every facet of our being, from the highest to the lowest, from the most spiritual to the most fleshly. We rightly seek adequate financial resources, sound health, stimulating work, respect from others, and so forth. Alas, it is all too tempting to spend our time chasing these and nothing else. To encourage these pursuits, then, is a bit redundant; like urging the globe to turn. Although the enneagram can help in these things, its principal function—as demonstrated in earlier chapters—is to address the deeper dimensions of life, where spirit and psyche meet.

Rightly understood, then, it offers us "a course in liberation," by freeing us from unconscious bondage to lesser entities and linking us instead to that which surpasses those entities, even as it clarifies and orders our relations to them. At its highest level, it mediates between transcendent and immanent, heaven and earth, vertical and horizontal. It is "too good a thing" to be relegated only to the everyday concerns of life, important though they are in their own right. At its best, it helps to attain "deeper" and "higher" forms of self-fulfillment. It moves us past horizontal wants and needs—even as it does not neglect them—and into the vertical dimensions in which our destinies find their completion.

In regard to the enneagram's spiritual or metaphysical applications, we must keep in mind the traditional anthropology discussed earlier, to wit: that we are triadic beings, composed of three basic elements: spirit, soul and body, or, in enneagram terms, essence, psyche and body. It is only in this way that we can clearly perceive the significance of the spiritual and transcendent ends of life over against the material and immanent ends. Furthermore, it allows us to see the role that freedom and power have in the spiritual life. What follows, then, consists of additional reflections on the interplay between the vertical and horizontal, or transcendent and immanent, aspects of life, and on how the enneagram can be used to attain and exercise spiritual freedom and power. Though many people understand freedom and power in relation to little other than material or "practical" ends, we shall apply them here to the higher planes of being which bear most directly on the enduring significance of our lives.

First, then, we suggest that such applications of freedom and power—to the spiritual rather than to the material planes alone—are in principle open to everyone, given a reasonable amount of intelligence and commitment. That is, unlike material desires, which in many cases are beyond the reach of all but a few, they are within the reach of nearly everyone. Clearly, not everyone can find the perfect career, or the perfect "significant other," or the perfect place to live, but nearly everyone can find his or her spiritual home, and, having found it, enjoy the freedom and power thenceforth available. Not that inner freedom and power are mere compensations for the allurements of the world; they offer, rather, the only *real* fulfillment there is, and, once found, the things that one would never give up, even for the world itself.

It is, after all, spirit and soul that define the essence of what it is to be human. All of the secondary desiderata—the fame, fortune and festivity that make the "world go round"—are ever in danger of loss, diminishment, or, if nothing else, falling victim to boredom, as do all material entities sooner or later. For the interest in material entities is more or less fleeting and secondary, and quickly loses meaning if detached from the deeper springs of life. Spirit and soul, by contrast, are linked to the supra-temporal domain. Soul, especially, is the indispensable link "here below," mediating spirit and matter, heaven and earth. For "Soul . . . is the locus of primary matter of secondary realities; soul the locus of things pre-eminently real, matter of things derivative from them; soul the locus of essential beings, matter of things that come to be by afterthought."[1]

As we are a composite of matter and spirit, body and soul, so we are scions of time and eternity, becoming and Being. We must consider freedom and power in relation to the spiritual realm and not to the material realm alone. To meet the needs of our composite nature, then, we advocate the paradigm of the "adept," that is, of the figure who combines the ethical aspirations of "sainthood" with the illuminated knowledge of the *gnostic*.[2] We advocate the man or

1. Proclus, *A Commentary on the First Book of Euclid's Elements*, Prologue Part 1 [12]–[15], translated by Glen R. Morrow (Princeton University Press, 1970).

2. As used here, "saint" does not refer to a perfect person in some popular or superficial sense, but to one who is consciously set apart for a special purpose, which is in fact the root meaning of the word. For its part, *gnostic* refers to a person

woman who combines both moral and intellectual qualities, faith and knowledge, effort and insight. Such a one parts company with modern paradigms by representing a combination of morality *and* gnosis ("illuminated" or spiritual knowledge) rather than morality alone, as is the contemporary preference. Morality alone is a vine without a root, colored by sentiment, untethered to cosmological and metaphysical realities. By combining the moral and the intellectual, the active and the contemplative, we can—like the adept— access the freedom and power that make it possible to stand athwart the spiritual ignorance of both ourselves and of the age in which we live.

We use the word "metaphysical" intentionally, as we have throughout these pages. This branch of knowledge, so named by Aristotle, treats of first principles by means of ontology and cosmology, as noted earlier. In doing so, it combines reason and intuition, the rational and the mystical. Though it combines the two, it is not limited to them; rather, it transcends them. As the domain of first principles, it relies on foundational truths made known by way of the "intellect," by which we refer to the spiritual capacity that bypasses discursive reason and apprehends truth directly, as does "essence" in enneagram usage.

That this capacity is real has been held by the great majority of the world's sages, and its enduring relevance has made it a major theme (along with the concept of orthodoxy) in this book, beginning with chapter one. In the traditional view, then, we have "an organ or faculty for the discernment of spiritual truth, which in its proper sphere, is as much to be trusted as the organs of sensation in theirs."[3] The existence of this organ is all but dismissed today, in the elite circles of Western societies. Even many varieties of New Age

---

in possession of "illuminated" or esoteric knowledge. As used here, it is not limited to, and is often at variance with, the Gnostic ideas of the early Christian period. In the words of Antoine Faivre, real *gnosis* refers to "an integrating knowledge, a grasp of fundamental relations ... that exist among the various levels of reality, e.g., among God, humanity and the universe." Quoted from *Access to Western Esotericism* (State University of New York Press, Albany, 1994), 19.

3. W.R. Inge, *Christian Mysticism* (Living Age Books, published by Meridian Books, New York, 1956), 6.

mysticism—many, not all—ignore it, preferring instead to stress experience and feeling to the exclusion of spiritual intuition, or intellect. Conventional forms of religion make equally few claims on the intellect, preferring instead to adapt their tenets to modernist paradigms—be they fundamentalist or liberal, or somewhere in between—and to make pronouncements on social and political issues. As a result, they entangle themselves in the very cosmic processes they should in fact work to overcome.

Inasmuch, then, as only the psycho-physical faculties are operative in the majority, "metaphysical truths will be made to seem more obscure than they are in themselves."[4] This is the case when people are unaware of spiritual realities, and of the intellect, specifically. Only by awareness of such realities, by way of intellect, can they consciously transcend in some measure the ebb and flow of psycho-physical life. Only then, can they "stand outside" themselves and examine, with discernment, the integrating and disintegrating dynamics of their souls. As one observer puts it, "Conscious beings live, almost by definition, outside of their bodies."[5] It is a matter, then, of becoming conscious of this distinction.

We must, then, be aware of the distinction between intellect and reason. Intellect is located in the domain of spirit or essence; reason, in the domain of soul or psyche. Reason, discursive reason, is the instrument for attaining practical ends. Intellect, on the other hand, probes the essence of things and processes, penetrating their hidden relationships and deeper meanings. In the words of Erich Fromm, intellect "is, as it were, not two-dimensional but 'perspectivistic' . . . it grasps all conceivable perspectives and dimensions, not only the practically relevant ones."[6]

An enneatype One, for example, is something more and other than the nitpicking, judgmental, conscientious, reforming and striving perfectionist that we see on the surface. He is that, of course. He can no more dispense with his ego, and the personality

4. Robert Bolton, *The Order of the Ages: World History in the Light of a Universal Cosmogony* (Sophia Perennis, San Rafael, CA, 2001), 189.
5. Robert Bolton, *Keys of Gnosis*, 11.
6. Ibid., quotation on page 31.

that represents it, than he can dispense with his body. Yet in his intellect, or "transpersonal nucleus," he stands outside the ego, above or beyond it, intuitively[7] observing and comprehending its dynamics, even as he stands outside his body, reflecting on its pains and pleasures, wants and needs. By contrast, his body does not observe or transcend his spirit. Spirit is the greater of the two.

Yet, how can this be? How can the spiritual be "greater" than the material? Indeed, more "real" or "concrete?" In Plotinus (whose *The Enneads* inspired Oscar Ichazo, seminal theorist of the enneagram of personality, despite his differences with the course of its development), the elevated position of spirit was firmly held. In his teaching, the spiritual domain is that which has authentic existence, and that which has it perfectly. The spiritual domain, or "Being," he asserted, "is Intellect, is wisdom unalloyed. . . . Hence its eternity, its identity, its utter . . . impermeability." Even so, he acknowledged, common sense held that things were otherwise. "Mountain and rock, the wide solid earth, all that resists," he observed, favored the greater reality of the corporeal plane, thus diminishing "entities like Soul and Intellect, things having no weight or pressure, yielding to no force . . . things not even visible?" Nonetheless, he argued, it is soul and Intellect that are substantial and lasting, unlike corporeal entities, whose "flux" and "perishing" testify to "their exclusion from the Kind whose Being is Authentic."[8]

Although we cite a classical source, in keeping with earlier examples, we find contemporary thinkers who make the same or a similar point. For instance, the neuroscientist Mario Beauregard maintains similar views in his excellent book, *The Spiritual Brain*. There, he and others harmonize empirical science with philosophy to make their case in a manner more congenial to modern minds. We do not gainsay this effort but praise it.

Another contemporary thinker, Robert Bolton, ruminates on

7. Intuitive knowing is not the product of vague feelings but the appropriation of first principles by the intellect, either in metaphysical form or as a "received doctrine" or religious revelation.

8. Plotinus, *The Enneads,* translated by Stephen McKenna (Penguin Books, London, 1991), Sixth Tractate, "The Impassivity of the Unembodied," III. 6, 194–196.

these and similar questions as well, but from a traditional perspective. In his view, the "common sense delusion is almost inevitable because the imagination is far more closely attached to the material level than reason is, and common sense typically tries to confine thought to what can be imagined." Yet, he says, intellect is exempt from dependence on sense and images. Hence, it is able to discover and define the real nature of material things. The preference of spiritual values, then, is "a choice of the greater concreteness and greater reality of the intelligible and unchanging instead of the material and the mutable." Happily, we may choose between greater and lesser values. The outcome will either "increase the power of the will by joining its activity to the greater reality, or . . . weaken it by joining it to the lesser reality." We assimilate ourselves, then, to that which most engages the will and the understanding, for good or ill; in other words, to that which is similar by nature to spirit and soul, or to that which is inferior to it.[9]

As indicated, the certitudes of intellect permit us to recognize and evaluate the ever-changing conditions of our psycho-physical being, of our "enneatypes," among other things. Stated otherwise, only the absolute can understand and interpret the relative. Empiricism provides truths about the psycho-physical world but not the spiritual world; only metaphysics—the science of first principles—is able to do the latter. By themselves, the partial and mutable qualities of the psycho-physical world yield relative truths and no more.

There is, in fact, absolute truth, but it can only be discerned by the intellect, the "lens of reality." By seeing through that lens, from the perspective of essence, we become objectively self-aware. We function from first principles, principles that underpin freedom and power. We reside at the center of the circle, mobilizing and integrating the mutable phenomena on the circumference. By contrast, if we function from a stance of relativity, external causes condition our minds and wills in proportion to our lack of awareness. Only through certitudes—knowledge of first principles that transcends the products of discursive reason—can we free ourselves to greater or lesser degrees from this conditioning.

9. *Keys of Gnosis*, 67.

The enneagram is a virtual encyclopedia of self-awareness, pointing toward both the transcendent domain—that is, toward essence—and toward the immanent domain—that is, towards psycho-physical realities. By it, we are reminded that unnoticed influences are often the most dangerous. Alerted to these, we are able to exert a benign influence over them, by refraining from actions prompted by internal and external stimuli. Those acquainted with enneatype know what this means. They recognize their weaknesses and blind spots, as well as their strengths and insights, and hence are superior to both. Knowledge is indeed power, in the inner as well as the outer worlds. By refraining from typical responses, we are freed from the penalties that would be imposed for giving in to them.

For example, by refusing to exert uncalled-for control over the lives of others, the Two is free to guide—and nourish—her own life; by refraining from the impulse to sample every superficial stimulant that presents itself, the Seven is free to deepen his experiences. By withdrawing energy, then, that would otherwise feed such responses, Twos, Sevens and other enneatypes channel it into beneficial forms of power. As in the first law of thermodynamics, energy is not destroyed; rather, it is directed to alternative uses; in this case, to spiritual purposes and values, thus allowing human beings a measure of causal and creative power. Unlike forms of power used to control other people and things, this power frees one to greater or lesser degrees from the bondage of social and natural pressures, from, we might say, social and material entities and their conditioning forces.

This is freedom indeed. It allows us to create our own identity, to "become who we are," to "individuate." As observed above, it allows us to function from our center, or essence, wherein we realize, with Aristotle, that attainment of spiritual wisdom renders material things secondary if not altogether unimportant.[10] By putting secondary things in their place, we gain power over them and freedom

10. This notion is common to all religions and many traditional philosophies. In the New Testament, for example, the disciples are urged to "seek first [God's] kingdom and his righteousness," after which their material needs will be met. (See Matthew 6:33).

in using them, a power and freedom unknown to those who give priority to them and who are, on that account, enslaved by them. Paradoxically, this power and freedom overflow from the spiritual into the material domain, providing an adequate or even abundant supply of material goods to persons who hold such goods to be of secondary importance.

As enneagram "adepts," we are equipped by knowledge that points to both transcendent and immanent planes of being. By way of intellect, by way, that is, of our transcendent and deiform center, we apprehend objectively not only spiritual truths but the thousand-and-one traits of personality that make us who we are as psycho-physical beings. This relationship between intellect and psyche, and the healing potentials inherent in it, are described by Frithjof Schuon, when he says:

> The great remedy for all our inward miseries is objectivity towards ourselves; and the source or starting point of this objectivity is situated above ourselves, in God. That which is in God is for that reason mirrored in our own transpersonal center which is the pure Intellect; that is, the Truth that saves us is part of our most intimate and most real substance.[11]

Just so. Being and becoming, transcendence and immanence; neither can be neglected without forfeiting our humanity; that is, forfeiting that which *surpasses* humanity.

Possession of the enneagram allows us to benefit both ourselves and others. Let us be grateful, then, for our privilege in having this practical and theoretical wisdom at hand even as we are willing to share it with anyone who wishes. As suggested earlier, let us be "wise as serpents and innocent as doves,"[12] members of a community that benefits society. For "the security of any society depends on the presence in it of minorities and individuals who are spiritually alien to it, who have a mission which goes far beyond the basic practicalities which rest on everyone. In their absence, disastrous events and changes can spread like the plague through populations whose

11. Frithjof Schuon, *Survey of Metaphysics and Esoterism*, 200.
12. Matthew 10:16.

collective will has become merged with natural forces."[13] Hence our vocation: to be salt and light, preservative and guide.

But to be of service, we must find and know ourselves, then surpass ourselves. We must, in the words of Dean Inge, "achieve inner *unity* by transcending mere individuality. The independent, imperious self shows its unreality by being inwardly discordant. [By being, that is, bound to basic fears, hidden complaints, characteristic temptations and cognitive errors.] It is of no use to enlarge the circumference of our life, if the fixed center is always the *ego*."[14]

Adepts of the enneagram, then, must cultivate intellect as the fixed center, the transpersonal core, the better to direct the variable experiences of the ego. Intellect, which links soul and spirit, is our proper center, however insignificant it may appear to the eyes of the senses, and in the calculus of material processes. Fortified, then, by spiritual freedom and power, we are content to bear the tensions between Being and becoming. We are, even, able to command nature, to varying degrees, because we are above it; we are able to direct the currents of the *inconstant* light, because we rest in the *constant* light.

13. *Keys of Gnosis*, 85.
14. *Christian Mysticism*, 33.

13

On Symbolism

There is no power in Nature like to that of Similitude. Everything draws and attracts its like to it.

                                              ~ Peter Sterry

As with a picture, so too a symbol: it is worth a thousand words. That is, if it is an authentic symbol. The enneagram appears to be such. Its curious geometry and mysterious origins, combined with its multiple applications, indicate that this is the case.

Like other symbols, it is an emblem, token or sign that represents something other than itself. In these pages, it represents the immaterial structure and dynamics of the psycho-spiritual self. In the view of G. I. Gurdjieff and others, it represents any number of additional processes.

Like other authentic symbols, symbols, that is, which are widespread and primordial, the enneagram serves principally as a means of internal communication.[1] It does so after the manner of symbols down through the ages, and, like them, it reflects primordial aspects of a psycho-spiritual nature. Unlike contrived symbols, the kind that are used to represent everything from commercial products to athletic teams, the enneagram, in its several versions, bears the stamp of other, more widely known symbols, such as the Tree of

---

1. It is, in large part, the synergy between visual symbol and verbal content that gives the enneagram its power. Other typologies, ranging from the ancient four humors theory to the modern Myers-Briggs theory, lack its all-important symbolic dimension. Though they offer much in regard to understanding personality, their lack of a complementary symbol renders them one-dimensional and hence lessens their impact. By contrast, the enneagram's combination of word and symbol stimulates both discursive reason and active imagination.

Life, the Rainbow, the All-Seeing Eye, the Cross, the Labyrinth, the Radiating Heart, the Sun, the Moon, the Cave, the Fish, the Wheel, and various other geometric patterns.

According to René Guénon, authentic or primordial symbols are "essentially synthetic" and thus intuitive, able to surpass words as support for intellectual intuition. As we have seen, intellectual intuition refers to a form of knowing that stands above or beyond words and reason, to a mode of understanding that prefigures and determines all lesser modes of understanding. In contrast, words and reason by themselves are confined largely to analytical and discursive understanding. Nonetheless, words contain an element of symbolism as well. Hence, there is no fundamental opposition between words and symbols; they are, rather, complementary.[2]

Unlike concepts limited to verbal content, the symbolism of which Guénon speaks opens the way to unlimited conceptual possibilities and meanings. Such symbols—the enneagram included, we believe—address not only persons skilled in abstract reasoning and dialectic, but anyone who is sensitive to the internal communication transmitted by such symbols. Authentic symbols, then, are specifically adapted to the capacities of human nature, which are not exclusively verbal and rational but which require "a sensory basis from which to raise itself to higher spheres."[3] This is because human beings are composite, one and multiple, not radically divided between soul and body as in Cartesian-based varieties of thought.

Symbols like the enneagram, then, are less narrowly defined than words. Hence, they are contingent and "accidental" in relation to the things they represent. To Hindus, for example, a statue may symbolize multiple aspects of the divinity, yet each aspect has the ability to serve as a reference point, aid or support for meditation. According to a Vedic text, such symbols "are like the horse which enables a man to make a journey more rapidly and with far less

---

2. René Guénon, *Symbols of Sacred Science*, 7. Guénon also observes that symbols and written language may be combined, as in certain forms of primitive "ideographic" writing.
3. Ibid., 7.

effort than if he had to make it on foot. No doubt, if this man had no horse he could still reach his destination, but with how much more difficulty! If he is able to make use of a horse, he would be quite wrong to refuse it on the pretext that it is more worthy not to have recourse to any aid."[4] Likewise, given enough time, a man might discover the patterns and dynamics of the psyche, but how much more speedily and accurately could he do so by using the enneagram.

Having explored to some extent the nature and use of authentic or primordial symbols, something should be said about their origin. In brief, we believe they are "non-human," that is, not the product of human imagination or ingenuity, although they clearly partake of human artistry in individual representations. According to traditional views, they originate by way of archetypal essence or energy, descend in condensed form to an imaginal symbol, and appear at last as a sensory symbol—such as an enneagram. It is a "top-down process;" the lower comes from the higher.

In our view, then, symbols are:

• Inherently appropriate,[5] that is, they are neither arbitrarily derived nor the result of convention, but rather possess an innate form that adequately expresses their meaning or meanings.
• Participants in a greater reality than themselves, that is, they grant access to levels of reality beyond everyday awareness, either horizontal or vertical.
• Able to translate energies between levels of reality, that is, to serve as agents of mediation between the interior and exterior, spiritual and physical domains.
• Able to serve as trans-rational agents, that is, as agents serving above and beyond rational functions.
• Polyvalent agents, that is, entities containing a variety of meanings (as indicated by Guénon above), thus allowing one to

4. Ibid., 8.
5. These criteria are drawn in large part from Nicholas Whitehead, *Patterns in Magical Christianity* (Sun Chalice Books, Albuquerque, NM, 1996), 16–24.

experience a wide range of related inner energies simultaneously.

These criteria are clearly applicable to the enneagram, which is,
we believe, neither arbitrary nor contrived but authentic, and which
lends itself to realities and processes both natural and supernatural.
In fact, so fertile is this symbol, according to Boris Mouravieff, that
its multiple aspects and meanings defeat attempts at categorization.
Indeed, he claims, citing a hyperbolic passage from the Gospel of
John, such aspects and meanings compare in quantity to the "things
that Jesus did," things which, if they had been recorded, he says
(agreeing with St. John), "The world itself could not contain the
books that would be written."[6] This is the case, he maintains, inasmuch as the enneagram

> contains the whole *Gnosis,* provides a kind of *universal instru-
> ment* that enables us to penetrate everything, providing, of
> course, that one uses it correctly in the search for Knowledge and
> Savoir-Faire. For example, with a single exception, all the sche-
> mata which appear in the volumes of 'Gnosis' [the author's mag-
> num opus] are derived from it, and, conversely, each of them
> reflects one or other of its aspects.... The traditional esoteric
> teaching is not concerned with the detailed description or com-
> mentary on these aspects or symbols, but with showing disciples
> how to use the universal instrument, provided in the enneagram,
> as a way of solving problems they are considering, whether these
> concern *being* or *action.*[7]

This may sound—indeed, may be—exaggerated, but so do Gurdi-
eff's similarly sweeping claims. One thing is certain: the enneagram
and its three fundamental elements, the circle, the equilateral triangle and the irregular hexagram—representing divine unity and
wholeness, the interaction of three forces, and process and develop-

---

6. Boris Mouravieff, *Gnosis: Book Three, The Esoteric Cycle, Study and Commentaries on the Esoteric Tradition of Eastern Orthodoxy* (Praxis Institute Press, Newburyport, Mass., 1993), 117–118. The citation is from John 21:25.
7. Ibid.

ment, respectively—do indeed embrace universal themes and concepts, and illustrate the dynamic interrelations between them.

The Art of Memory, by Francis A. Yates,[8] contains additional material regarding primordial symbolism and, indirectly, the enneagram. Following the lead of Thomist and Dominican theorists, she agrees that sensible phenomena—those things that are visible, audible, and so forth—are more retainable in the memory than intelligible phenomena. Moreover, she continues, the new, the odd, the unusual and the striking accentuate the retainable aspects of phenomena. Clearly, the enneagram fits these criteria, with the exception of newness. Even then, it appears to be new to virtually everyone who encounters it. Thus, in keeping with earlier observations, the enneagram's "sensible" aspect gives it an edge over merely mental phenomena, including typologies that are essentially verbal.

In her pioneering work, Yates devoted many pages to Giordano Bruno (1548–1600), a Dominican friar much given to the use of "seals" and other symbolic diagrams (and who was mentioned in the introductory chapter). He was convinced that such diagrams reflect psycho-spiritual realities. Indeed, he believed such "inner images . . . are nearer to reality than the objects of the outer world, that [in them] reality is grasped and unified vision achieved."[9] Moreover, he believed such symbols attract both celestial and demonic powers, that is, sources and impulses of virtue and vice.[10] He drew and meditated on numerous such symbols. These mandala-like structures, for such they were, served as tools to facilitate self-development, as mirrors to reflect levels of self-consciousness, and even as "instruments for transforming demonic forces."

In all of these things, Bruno was a devotee of Raymond Lull (1233–1315), the Franciscan philosopher and mathematician (who was also mentioned in the introductory chapter). Lull, too, employed

---

8. Francis A. Yates, *The Art of Memory* (The University of Chicago Press, Chicago, IL, and Routledge and Kegan Paul, London, 1974).

9. Ibid., 299.

10. Ibid., 293.

a variety of symbols in his *Ars Magna* and *Ars Brevis,* including enneagrams (more complex than the ones today) and "combinatory wheels." Moreover, he posited nine vices, nine virtues, and nine "Dignities of God," notions that clearly resonate with today's enneagram. In addition, he represented "movement in the psyche" on the revolving wheels of his images, a revolutionary concept at the time, and his diagrams, figures and schematizations in general served as "a kind of visual memory" aimed at increasing virtue and decreasing vice. By adapting elements of the Lullian art, Bruno sought to locate "a really operative organization of the psyche" by using images to harmonize "the changing forms of elemental nature within the psyche."[11]

As mentioned above, there are broader applications of primordial symbols, for example, to nature as a whole. This makes the most sense if the universe is in fact the creation of the Divine Word or Logos; the creation, that is, of a Being or Principle who is Source and Sustainer of all that is. If everything that is has its principle in the Divine principle, then everything—actual or symbolic—is represented or translated by that Principle, according to its own order of existence, from one order of being to another, with all things linked to and corresponding on various levels of being. According to René Guénon, such correspondences are the basis of symbolism and the reason why laws of a lower domain "may always be taken as symbolizing realities of a higher order," from which they draw their existence.[12] Therefore Sun, Moon, Wheel, Labyrinth, and so forth, serve as symbols of higher realities. So, too, does the enneagram, which reflects macrocosmic and metacosmic attributes in the spirit and soul of the human microcosm. It links, therefore, a primordial symbol of non-human origin to the psycho-spiritual realities of human life.

According to Boris Mouravieff, as noted earlier, traditional teachings surrounding the enneagram are best employed in "showing disciples how to use the universal instrument ... as a way of solving

11. *The Art of Memory,* 176, 186, 178, 249, 251.
12. *Symbols of Sacred Science,* 10.

problems they are considering, whether these concern *being* or *action*."[13] This is a gift to persons inhabiting the fragmented and scattered spiritual landscape of the present day. The gift is made possible by two entities working synergistically: the symbol we have been discussing, and the body of psycho-spiritual teaching that complements it. Together, these entities encompass a power of understanding and healing found in few other places.

13. *Gnosis*, 118.

Afterword

We are here at a given point on the mighty wheel, not elsewhere. If we are here, it is because God has placed us here.

~A.G. Sertillanges

A S WE HAVE SEEN, the enneagram provides a valuable symbol on which to trace the features of human personality. Based on correspondence between symbol and psyche, it serves as mirror and hieroglyph, as subtle means of unveiling otherwise hidden phenomena.

Despite our enthusiasm, Valentin Tomberg, in his finest work, raises questions about similar techniques.[1] In the passage we have in mind, in which he addresses "practical Hermeticism" (a discipline not unrelated to enneagram theory) he declares there is "nothing mechanical or surgical" in the work of inner development.[2] He makes it clear he prefers an "organic" method. "This means to say," he explains, "that one will not find any kind of device within [Hermeticism]—mental, ceremonial or physiological—by means of which one would be able to know and accomplish things surpassing . . . the moral and intellectual faculties that one possesses."

He allows that "devices" of self-development, be they the pronunciation of mantric syllables, controlled breathing, or intellectual techniques, may confer "temporary advantages" but that in the end they reach an impasse. As examples, he recommends against using the *ars combinatoria* ("the art of combination") of Raymond Lull and the "archeometry" of Saint-Yves Alveydre, "ingenious and well-

---

1. *Meditations on the Tarot: A Journey Into Christian Hermeticism* (Jeremy P. Tarcher/Putnam, New York, 1985), 452.
2. Hermeticism pertains generally to the occult sciences, such as alchemy and astrology, especially in regard to doctrines ascribed to the legendary Hermes Trismegistus. In Tomberg's work, the term is defined and expounded as *Christian* Hermeticism.

founded though they are." In place of these, he urges development of spiritual and magical "ferments" or "enzymes" of thought, which he finds natural and non-programmatic.

We refer to this passage not to take issue with it, for it contains much sound wisdom, as does his book as a whole, but as a departure point to observe that such "instruments of thought," though by nature limited in their utility, are of assistance in achieving the results sought after in these pages. It is interesting that Tomberg should have referenced Raymond Lull, for in fact Lull was, in his *Ars Combinatoria,* the developer of proto-enneagrams and personality systems. Such systems do, we believe, open to many minds a mode of knowing that is otherwise inaccessible, for they use both visual symbol and verbal content in creative and penetrating ways. They provide openings to inner dimensions of personality, as well as to religious and spiritual understandings, that may otherwise remain closed.

For some, or perhaps many persons, use of the enneagram or a similar "instrument of thought" is well nigh a necessity, "without which their faith would be empty and unstable."[3] We especially believe this to be true today, owing to the general absence of both traditional esoteric and exoteric metaphysics. The enneagram, based as it is on traditional insights delivered in a present-day idiom, goes some distance in remedying that absence.

That said, we do not claim the enneagram as a panacea for all that ails us. It cannot remedy what Thomas De Quincey called the "wounds that will not heal," wounded parts of psyche and spirit that must await the "final trump" before the pain ceases. For there is in such pain a Providential message, a reminder that the slings and arrows of individual destiny have a role to play in molding us into the persons that God wants us to be.

In relation to this, we recall the patriarch Jacob, who wrestled against God at the River Jabbok, earning a blessing, a new name, and . . . a dislocated hip, a wound that did not heal, a perpetual reminder of the night he had striven with God and prevailed. Then

3. Robert Bolton, *Self and Spirit,* 7. In this passage, the author is not speaking of the enneagram but of his own Traditionalist philosophy, which is, we believe, congenial to enneagram theory.

there is St. Paul, who suffered a "thorn in the flesh" in spite of, indeed, because of, his mystical experiences, to keep him humble and reliant on grace. Nor can we forget the origin of Eve, in the earliest pages of the Bible, born from a wound in Adam's side, prefiguring the alternately suffering and triumphing *ecclesia*, itself born from a wound in Christ's side. Nor let us forget that Christ himself retained—indeed, retains—in his glorified body the wounds of his Passion, not only in his side but in his head, hands and feet.

Moreover, to this day, there are certain pious Jews who do not paint a room without leaving a small patch of it uncovered, to remind them there is no finality in this life, no heavenly rescue from imperfect existence, no earthly balm for the wounds that will not heal. In like manner, the saved will bear the wounds of their earthly journey, both here and hereafter. Only God is perfect, yet even he, in the person of the Son, retains his wounds.

How can this be? How does it fit into God's plan? How can the Giver of all good gifts subject his followers to a life leavened with "fear and trembling," to deliver them, after a series of trials and temptations, only at the last? Yet Holy Writ has it so: "I form light and create darkness, I make weal and create woe; I the LORD do all these things" (Isaiah 45:7).

It is a fact that human beings can conceive of no existence, holy or unholy, profane or celestial, that is not built of contrast: pleasure and pain, white and black, up and down, right and wrong. The benefits of grace are tempered by distress. One feels happiness only after knowing sadness; one feels pleasure only in the wake of pain.

Imagine you have been seriously injured in an accident, thus pitching you from the normal range of feelings into a state of pain and fear. Let us say you remain in that state for a period of time, praying for relief, escape, oblivion. Emergency personnel arrive at last, dispensing reassurance, tending your wounds, producing a longed-for dose of morphia. No greater contrast can be imagined. Within minutes of receiving an injection, the consuming pain begins to ebb; the oppressive mood begins to lift. Euphoria prevails, mentally and physically, polar opposite of the preceding state of misery. Until such time as the effects begin to wane, you experience the most exquisite pleasure, from the drug's properties and by contrast with the earlier agony. So it goes: pleasure and pain, black and white, weal and woe. A parallel narrative could be applied to psychological pain, as well. Light and dark, good and bad, then, whether physical or mental, remain the poles of human existence, and will remain so until the tears of our eyes have been dried (Revelation 21:4), and the wolf and the lamb live together. (Isaiah 11:6).

As indicated, the wound that will not heal has a Providential purpose. In the schema of the enneagram, there is a psychic wound at the core of our personality type and of our type's compensating strategies. To counter the presence and pain of the wound, the various types marshal the passions peculiar to their natures, be they pride, deceit, envy, greed, fear, gluttony, lust, sloth or anger. In however obvious or subtle a manner, these passions are deployed as psychological defenses to protect from the dangers posed by the world. Yet the wound is something more than a festering presence, good only to keep us on our toes against threats to our egocentric selves. It serves as well as the focal point of a coalescing complex of virtues, sparked into life by the necessity to recognize, analyze, understand and in time transcend the wound, all the while remaining aware of the wound's continuing presence and necessity. The process creates a pearl of great price. The wound is the grain of sand in the shell of an oyster, an irritant about which forms a lustrous and finely colored gem. The wound is a passion around which forms a human personality of dignity and beauty, if that wound is understood, accepted, and overcome despite residual effects.

In summary, the enneagram is expert at bringing balance, insight and integration to soul and spirit, to recognizing and treating the wounds that will not heal, to providing a method of living productively and meaningfully despite one's wounds. Though it will never provide its adepts a perfect life, never heal every hurt, never banish every shadow, it provides all the same an effective antidote to any number of interior maladies. In doing so, it sometimes seems like a bit of "white magic." Magic is an applied science, indeed, the science of the Magi, and the enneagram—by disciplines of insight and integrity imposed upon its adepts—does indeed help transmute one's psychological contents. It is this alchemy of the soul that makes it special, and that works its magic to such effect.

Bibliography

Benoist, Alain de, *On Being a Pagan*. Translated by Jon Graham, edited by Greg Johnson, ULTRA, Atlanta, GA, 2004.

Berry, Ray, editor, *The Spiritual Athlete: A Primer for the Inner Life*. Joshua Press, Olema, CA, 1992.

Bolton, Robert, *Keys of Gnosis*. Sophia Perennis, Hillsdale, NY, 2004.

_____, *The Order of the Ages: World History in the Light of a Universal Cosmogony*, Sophia Perennis, San Rafael, CA, 2001.

_____, *Person, Soul and Identity: A Neoplatonic Account of the Principle of Personality*. Minerva Press, London, 1994

_____, *Self and Spirit*. Sophia Perennis, Hillsdale, NY, 2005.

Bonhoeffer, Dietrich, *The Cost of Discipleship*. MacMillan Publishing Co., Inc., NY, 1963.

Bonner, Anthony, and Eve Bonner, editors, translators, *Doctor Illuminatus: A Ramon Lull Reader*. Princeton University Press, Princeton, NJ, 1993.

Borella, Jean, "The Problematic of the Unity of Religions." *Sacred Web: A Journal of Tradition and Modernity,* volume 17, North Vancouver, British Columbia, Canada, June 2006.

_____, *The Secret of the Christian Way: A Contemplative Ascent Through the Writings of Jean Borella*. Editor and translator, G. John Champoux, State University of New York Press, Albany, 2001.

Bridges, Jerry, *The Pursuit of Holiness*. NavPress, Colorado Springs, 1989.

Bullinger, E.W., *Number in Scripture*. Kregel Publications, Grand Rapids, MI, 1967.

Carnell, Corbin Scott, *Bright Shadow of Reality: C. S. Lewis and the Feeling Intellect*. William B. Eerdmans Publishing Company, Grand Rapids, MI, 1974.

Chesterton, G.K., *Orthodoxy*. Image Books, Garden City, NY, 1959.

Cohen, Edmund D., *C.G. Jung and the Scientific Attitude*. Philosophical Library, NY, 1975.

Evagrius Ponticus, *The Praktikos* and *Chapters On Prayer*. Translated by John Eudes Bamberger, OCSO, Cistercian Publications, Kalamazoo, MI, 1981.

Fabre d'Olivet, *The Golden Verses of Pythagoras*. Translated by Nayán Louise Redfield, Bibliobazaar, LaVergne, TN, 2009.

Faivre, Antoine, *Access to Western Esotericism*. State University of New York Press, Albany, 1994.

Fohr, Samuel D., *Adam & Eve: The Spiritual Symbolism of Genesis and Exodus*. Sophia Perennis, Hillsdale, NY, 2001.

Franz, Marie-Louise von, *Alchemical Active Imagination*. Shambala, Boston, MA, 1997.

Guénon, René, *Symbols of Sacred Science*. Translated by Henry D. Fohr, Sophia Perennis, Ghent, NY, 1995.

_____, *Perspectives on Initiation*. Translated by Henry D. Fohr, edited by Samuel D. Fohr, Sophia Perennis, Ghent, NY, 2001.

Hallesby, Ole, *Temperament and the Christian Faith*. Augsburg Publishing House, Minneapolis, MN, 1962.

Horney, Karen, *Neurosis and Human Growth: The Struggle Toward Self-Realization*. W.W. Norton and Company, Inc., NY, 1991.

Huxley, Aldous, *The Perennial Philosophy*. Harper & Row Publishers, Inc., NY, 1944.

Inge, William R., *Christian Mysticism*. Meridian Books, NY, 1956.

Isham, Thomas Garrett, *Dimensions of the Enneagram: Triad, Tradition, Transformation*. The Lion and the Bee, Marshall, MI, 2004.

James, William, *Varieties of Religious Experience*. Penguin Books, NY, 1986.

Jung, Carl Gustav, *Psychological Types*. Princeton University Press, Princeton, NJ, 1971.

Kant, Immanuel, *Anthropology from a Pragmatic Point of View*. Translated by Victor Lyle Dowdell, Southern Illinois University Press, Carbondale and Edwardsville, IL, 1996.

Kaufmann, Walter, *Without Guilt and Justice: From Decidophobia to Autonomy*. Dell Publishing Co., Inc., NY, 1973.

Larchet, Jean-Claude, *Mental Disorders and Spiritual Healing: Teachings from the Early Christian East*. Translated by Rama P. Coomaraswamy and G. John Champoux, Sophia Perennis, Hillsdale, NY, 2005.

Lévi, Eliphas, *The History of Magic*. Translated by A.E. Waite, Samuel Weiser, Inc., York Beach, ME, 2000.

Lewis, C.S., *The Discarded Image: An Introduction to Medieval and Renaissance Literature*. Cambridge University Press, UK, 1998.

_____, *Letters to Malcolm: Chiefly on Prayer*. Harcourt Brace Jovanovich, New York and London, 1964.

_____, *George MacDonald, An Anthology*. Macmillan, 1947.

Machen, J. Gresham, *What is Faith?* The Banner of Truth Trust, Edinburgh, 1991.

Maistre, Joseph de, *The Works of Joseph de Maistre*. Translated by Jack Lively, MacMillan, 1965.

Mouravieff, Boris, *Gnosis: Study and Commentaries on the Esoteric Tradition of Eastern Orthodoxy*, Book three, Esoteric Cycle. Translated by Maneck d'Oncieu, Praxis Institute Press, Newburyport, MA, 1993.

Mullens, E.Y., *The Axioms of Religion*. The Judson Press, Philadelphia, 1908.

Bibliography

Naranjo, Claudio, *Ennea-Type Structures: Self-Analysis for the Seeker.* Gateways/IDHHB, 1990.

Nee, Watchman, *The Spiritual Man.* Christian Fellowship Publishers, Inc., NY, 1977.

Oldham, John M., and Lois B. Morris, *Personality Self-Portrait: Why You Think, Work, Love and Act the Way You Do.* Bantam Books, NY, 1991.

Packer, J.I., *Concise Theology: A Guide to Historic Christian Beliefs.* Tyndale House Publishers, Inc., Wheaton, IL, 1993.

_____, *I Want to Be a Christian.* Tyndale, 1977.

_____, *Knowing God.* Intervarsity Press, Downers Grove, IL, 1973.

_____, *Rediscovering Holiness.* Servant Publications, Ann Arbor, Mich., 1992.

_____, and Carolyn Nystrom, *Never Beyond Hope: How God Touches & Uses Imperfect People.* Intervarsity, 2000.

Pascal's Pensées. E.P. Dutton & Co., Inc., NY, 1958.

Perry, Whitall N., *The Spiritual Ascent: A Compendium of the World's Wisdom.* Fons Vitae, Louisville, KY, 2000.

Plato, *Timaeus 90, The Dialogues of Plato.* Translated by Benjamin Jowett, William Benton, publisher, Encyclopaedia Britannica, Inc., Chicago, 1952.

Plotinus, *The Enneads,* Sixth Tractate, "The Impassivity of the Unembodied," III. Translated by Steven McKenna, Penguin Books, London, 1991.

Proclus, *A Commentary on the First Book of Euclid's Elements,* Prologue Part I. Translated by Glen R. Morrow, Princeton University Press, Princeton, NJ, 1970.

Riso, Don Richard, with Russ Hudson, *Personality Types, Using the Enneagram for Self-Discovery.* Houghton Mifflin Co., Boston, NY, 1996.

Rohr, Richard, and Andreas Ebert, *Discovering the Enneagram: An Ancient Tool for a New Spiritual Journey.* The Crossroad Publishing Company, NY, 1992.

Ryle, J. C., *Holiness.* Evangelical Press, Darlington, England, 1999.

Schuon, Frithjof, *Survey of Metaphysics and Esoterism.* Translated by Gustavo Polit, World Wisdom Books, Bloomington, IN, 1986.

_____, *Understanding Islam.* World Wisdom Books, Inc., 1998.

_____, *The Eye of the Heart.* World Wisdom Books, Inc., 1997.

Singer, Dorothea Waley, *Giordano Bruno: His Life and Thought.* Henry Schuman, NY, 1950.

Stafford, William S., *Disordered Loves: Healing the Seven Deadly Sins.* Cowley Publications, Boston, MA, 1994.

Tomberg, Valentin, *Meditations on the Tarot: A Journey Into Christian Hermeticism.* Jeremy F. Tarcher/Putnam, NY, 2002.

Whitehead, Nicholas, *Patterns in Magical Christianity.* Sun Chalice Books, Albuquerque, NM, 1996.

Whyte, Alexander, *The Treasury of Alexander Whyte.* Baker Book House, Grand Rapids, MI, 1968.

Wilber, Ken, *The Marriage of Sense and Soul.* Shambala Publications, Boston, MA, 2001.

Wiltse, Virginia, and Helen Palmer, "Hidden in Plain Sight: Observations on the Origins of the Enneagram. 2011 *Enneagram Journal.* Cincinnati, OH.

Yates, Frances A., *The Art of Memory.* The University of Chicago Press, 1974.

Index of Names

Index of Names

www.ingramcontent.com/pod-product-compliance
Lightning Source LLC
Chambersburg PA
CBHW022008090426
42741CB00007B/938